Hildebrand: The Builder

By

ERNEST ASHTON SMITH, Ph. D.
Professor of History, Allegheny College

CINCINNATI: JENNINGS AND GRAHAM
NEW YORK: EATON AND MAINS

18524

To My Mother.

CONTENTS

I. The Times of the Builder, - - - 7

II. The Evolution of an Institution, - 23

III. The Condition of the Clergy, - - 39

IV. The Sway of the German Popes, - 55

V. The-Corner Stone of Papal Freedom, 73

VI. The Power Behind the Papal See, - 87

VII. The Plan of the Master Builder, - 103

VIII. The Challenge by the Church, - 126

IX. The Climax at Canossa, - - - 144

X. The Encounter With the Empire, - 157

XI. The Hildebrandine Epistles, - - 183

XII. The Man and His Mission, - - 202

CHAPTER I.

THE TIMES OF THE BUILDER.

SUTRI, anciently known as the Key of Etruria, holds, with its compact stone structures, the entire crest of one of the elevations that border the plains of Central Italy. From it, range after range of delicate mountain distance is discernible. Volscian, Sabine, and Alban Hills, with Soracte, sung by Horace, nobly beautiful, rise out of the soft, quiet lines of Campagna, while the Tiber winds away out of the meadow-lands until it is lost from sight before it reaches Rome, thirty miles to the south. In this cliff-perched town, as first in territorial proximity within the Patrimonium Petri, there was held on December 20, 1046, one of the momentous Councils molding the relations between the Church and the State. Henry the Third, the strongest and the ablest in the line of German kings, had made with majesty and splendor a first visit to his Italian possessions. Boniface, Margrave of Tuscany, the leading prince of the land, tendered magnificent receptions. The Imperial Court convened at Piacenza.

But the more urgent business of the time

7

was a call from the Archdeacon Peter, of the Church Universal, for the Cæsar from beyond the Alps to intervene in the tangled affairs of the Papacy. Its demoralized condition was rather inelegantly set forth in the statement that the Church had three husbands. Benedict IX performed his ministrations at the Church of St. John Lateran, Gregory VI at St. Peter's, and Sylvester III at Santa Maria Maggiore. The first of these Popes was the relative and creature of the Tusculum counts, the masters of the Roman nobility. Elevated to the supreme office of the Church, just before he entered his teens, the following dozen years of his life were given to bringing foul disgrace upon the sacred duties of his position. The populace had for very shame's sake driven him away and chosen a second Pope in the person of John of Sabina, who took the title of Sylvester III. Benedict was disposed at first to acquiesce, being eager to marry a young woman of the city. Disappointed in this venture, his powerful friends helped him to assume again the tiara.

The third disputant for authority was in many respects a worthy man, of a certain purity of intention, and he represented in curious contradiction the struggling forces which were to reform the Papacy. John Gratian, the rich archpriest of the St. John at the Lateran Gate, had bought deliberately from Benedict IX the title of Pope, taking the name of Gregory VI. The bargain was freely applauded by Peter Damiani and the adherents of the Cluniac movement. It was hailed as an omen of better times. But the vender of holy things seemed to rue the trade, since in two years Gregory had secured little actual authority, though resorting to aggressive measures, while pillage, disorder, sacrilege, and general insecurity prevailed in the Papal territory.

At Sutri then, accordingly, a Council of Bishops and Roman clergy, in company with King Henry, heard the claims of the three rivals. Benedict anticipated action in his case by resigning a second time. Sylvester was removed by the Council even from his priestly office, and sentenced to life imprisonment in a convent. Gregory VI, by virtue of his office, had the presiding seat in the assembly, and, in the absence of any procedure of impeachment, the bishops quite cleverly asked this remaining contestant to describe the method by which he secured his election. The simple narrative revealed the glaring impropriety of his elevation, so that Gregory impulsively and honestly exclaimed: "In doing what I did, I hoped to obtain the forgiveness of my sins and the grace of God. But now I see the snare into which the enemy has trapped me. Tell me what I must do." The bishops could answer simply, "Judge thyself," adding the exhortation: "It will be better for thee to live like the holy Peter, poor in this world and to be blessed in another, than like the magician Simon, whose example misled thee, to shine in riches here and receive hereafter the sentence of condemnation." The thoroughly penitent Gregory then proclaimed: "I, Gregory, bishop, servant of servants of God, pronounce that on account of the heretical simony which took place at my election, I am deposed of the Roman See." The Council acquiesced, and adjourned to Rome.

However, now it is to be noted that, in the record of this assembly, there first appears in the public history of the affairs of the Church and the Empire the name of Hildebrand. This man was apparently a humble clerk in the household of Gregory VI, but his influence henceforth in all ecclesiastical relations for the succeeding forty years was to be continuous, and ultimately absolute. In direct defiance of the judgment passed at Sutri upon his master as a usurper, and in high loyalty to him, Hildebrand will later assume designedly the title of Gregory VII. A Synod of twenty-four prelates met in St. Peter's on December 22, 1046, and there was directed by Henry III to elect a Pope. The Romans protested that they did not possess the right of choice, and declaring the German sovereign the Patricius of Rome, they asked him to name the new successor of St. Peter. Henry III had been received into the city with extravagant acclaims of joy. Never before or since was there a foreign ruler so welcomed to the world's capital. He thereupon assumed the green mantle, the golden circlet, and the ring, emblematic of the Patriciate, and took by the hand Suidger, Bishop of Bamberg, who became Clement II.

This German Churchman had the religious spirit and fervor of his liege lord. Henry, by his second marriage with Agnes, the daughter of William of Aquitaine, had come into close political alliance with the program of the congregation of Cluny. He had acquired Burgundy, and thus received a powerful incentive to introduce the reforms demanded by the Order, both at Rome and in Germany. In January, 1047, a Council met at the call of Clement II, and condemned in the strongest terms the widely prevalent practice of simony. But its censure could not be strictly applied, and instead of the summary degradation of those guilty of the sacrilege, the penalty was a forty days' penance. Thus a new epoch in Papal history was inaugurated, and the incidents of this crisis give a suggestive, illuminating view of some of the forces and conditions which mark the period.

The elections of the Holy See were without fixed rule or requirement. A city faction, a combination of clergy, a group of nobility, or a territorial party might be the constituency. Simony was the great evil everywhere manifest in the succession of clerical offices, even invoked by John Gratian, as above related, in the hope of bringing good to pass out of bad. In the mutual relations of Church and State the Empire was clearly the dominant force. The German rulers had supplied

the element of reform more than once when the
Church was in utter demoralization. The surrender to Henry III left no bound to the imperial
power in Rome. This sovereign's mind had no
conception but that of the feudal relation, and
while he respected the majesty of the Church, he
believed the Pope should be directly bound by the
authority of the civil throne. An ambitious and
powerful Pope was sure to antagonize such a claim.
Henceforth there is clearly foreshadowed the
mighty struggle of the investiture.

The eleventh century was indeed to witness a
marvelous transformation in the majesty and the
authority of the official organization of the Roman
Church. Its new height of power has been a chief
argument by its adherents for its supernatural
and illimitable rights. The circumstances under
which this ecclesiasticism took on a new and full
life must be well comprehended at the beginning
of this study. The social and political environment
was of the very essence of mediævalism. It is
true that the idea of imperialism and centraliza-
tion given by Charlemagne to Europe in 800 A. D.
was not destined to perish, for the claim of wide
sovereignty asserted by Otto the Great, after an
interval of a century and a half, was a pledge of
the principle of nationality that would ultimately
prevail. But the tendencies of the past were yet
in the eleventh century all powerful, and feudalism
flourished at its height.

Europe was divided into hundreds of small territories, independent of one another, each having its own ruler, army, coinage, laws, and customs. There was no compact, homogeneous France, Italy, or Germany. The last State consisted of a score of larger duchies and principalities, and a multitude of margraviates, landgraviates, and bishoprics, many of them of petty significance in population and actual power. In addition, the continent was broken up into an apparently infinite number of tribes and tongues. There were Saxons, Suabians, Frisians, Franks, Czechs, Slavs, Moravians, and a host of others east of the Rhine. In the west, France could show almost as varied an assortment. Italy was a turmoil of Lombard, Tuscan, Norman, and Greek; so that Europe at large seemed to be in a condition of utter incoherence. Nevertheless, the stirrings of a new political order were to be felt within the hundred years. In England, Canute had caught the spirit of the coming ages, and, as the real organizer of Denmark, Sweden, and Norway, had his visions of a four-parted empire.

The son and grandson of the founder of the new French dynasty of the Capetians held sway for more than half of the eleventh century. But the royal domain was very scanty, having for its chief content the ancient foundation of Isle de France, along the Seine, in the region of Paris. Just as powerful rulers as Robert II and Henry I were the feudatory counts and dukes of Brittany,

Normandy, Flanders, Gascony, Toulouse, and Champagne.

Spain was yet in embryo, but Portugal had seceded from Castile into an autonomous existence. Leon and Castile formed a temporary union, which, after a period of separation, brought completed statehood. Navarre and Aragon were of shifting importance, while the Moors strongly held the south of the peninsula. Poland, in the valley of the Vistula, had just entered into the international Christian fellowship, under its able ruler Boleslas, through its acceptance of the orthodox religion; and Hungary, renouncing its Turanian antecedents, had completed its astounding transformation under the sovereign who abandoned the old name of Waik, and sought baptism into the Roman communion as Stephen. No uniformity of national advance existed in this period, though in various ill-expressed forms Europe had assumed the outlines familiar to modern eyes.

Easily first, Germany took the leadership by virtue of the revival of the Holy Roman Empire. Voltaire's arraignment that the so-named State was neither Roman nor holy would leave little possibility of a political entity, but the German foundation had its full measure of reality, in so far as consistent with the feudal disposition of the Teuton. Granted that the Holy Roman Empire was more of a shadow than a substance, the ideal it embodied is the clue to the activities and ambitions of the successive dynasties of Saxon, Franconian, and Hohenstaufen rulers. In the main, they had vigorous support in their immediate native possessions. To the kingly scepter of Germany was added the iron crown of the Lombards at Milan. Then the imperial diadem, bestowed at Rome, completed the most majestic authority of the age and the continent. In practical statesmanship, Henry III had proven himself a worthy successor to the noblest Cæsar of classic days. But this imperial sway included two remote, dissimilar, and uncongenial peoples. The absence of a German ruler from Italy meant opportunity for the ambitions of the most restless elements in Christendom. The succession of a new emperor was usually marked by a bitter contest for the control of Italy. Many feudal barons acknowledged only under compulsion the Northern master, and the Saracens held fast to the south of Italy and to Sicily. The Crescentii ruled in Sabina, the Sequi in Campagna, but the mightiest figure at the middle of the eleventh century was Boniface of Tuscany, the grandson of Ezzo, Lord of Canossa. His father, Tedald, had secured Ferrara, Mantua, Modena, and Brescia. The favor of the emperor gave Boniface the possessions of Rainer of Tuscany, with marriage to Beatrice, daughter of Frederick, Duke of Upper Lorraine, one of the two immortal heroines of the Hildebrandine contest.

Interest centers in the city of Rome, whose government was a close senatorial body that held the magistracy and judicial powers. There was no higher class strong enough to form the basis of a secular constitution. The Papacy had its program, which was hostile to civic progress. The nobles exercised the real power, and they contended with both emperor and Pope. The ruling force was supplied by the Tusculum family. The stronghold of this house, older than Rome itself, was fifteen miles distant from Rome. Here was the seat of Cicero's Academy, and the villa that gave to literature the Tusculan Disputations. From this impregnable town its counts had lorded it over the Latin mountains and part of Campagna, and the masters of the eleventh century claim direct descent from the mighty Alberic, last senator of Rome, and the infamous Marozia. They furnished the candidates either for the Papacy or the tyranny of the civil government of Rome. The Eternal City at this epoch, according to the account of Gregorovius, bore mute but eloquent testimony to the ravages of rival parties and unending warring factions. The narrow, irregular streets wore a gloomy, threatening appearance. The dwellings, of rough exterior and fortress like, arose on the foundations of classic sites. The relics of antiquity, splendid columns of Corinthian and Ionic patterns, were used to decorate these mansions. No protection was afforded to the ruins of theaters, arches, and baths.

Fish were exposed for sale on blocks of rarest

marble, once the seats of the mightiest rulers. The sarcophagi of heroes served as cisterns and troughs. The churches were foremost in appropriating the plunder of past grandeur and beauty. Citadels of offense and defense were constructed here and there by the contending nobles, while the poor lived among the vaults and recesses of foundations. The Palatine was a show-place, with its colossal remains of the imperial palaces. The Quirinal, Viminal, and Esquiline Hills contained a minor portion of dwellings, but the Cœlian and the Aventine were thickly populated. Streets were named for churches and for monuments. The Via Lata was the most splendid quarter. The Via Pontificalis ran through the Field of Mars to St. Peter's. This church, with the castle of St. Angelo, was beyond the Tiber, and comprised what was known as the Leonine City.

However varied and distinctive is this survey of territory, nation, race, and government, these years after the first Christian millennium furnish an array of names that compare favorably with those of other early centuries. There were the firm-hearted, erudite Lanfranc; the loyal, orthodox Anselm, Abbot of Bec; Urban II, the herald of the heroic Crusades; William the Conqueror, the maker of the larger England; Sancho the Great; Alphonso, the ruler of Castile and Leon, and the legendary Cid Campeador. This is the age of the sturdy, artistic Norman cathedral-builder, the

2

epoch of the series of monastic revolutions, the
Cluniacs, the Camaldules, the Cistercians, and the
Carthusians.

But these worthies and reformers make but a
background to the greatest figure of all. One
genius plays the part that stamps him for all time
among earth's mightiest. Hildebrand is the name
most potent of his age, and with the greatest post-
humous influence by reason of his deeds. Few
historical characters have had such conflicting accounts of their lives and deeds. Every contem-
porary writer was a partisan for or against the
policy of this revolutionist. The same controversy
descends to modern times, and it is doubtful if a
unanimity of judgment has yet been reached. The
fame of his later life cast back preternatural splendor on his early days, and his chroniclers have furnished a mass of material that is for the most part
untrustworthy.

Hildebrand was born probably in 1018, in or
near Saona, a town at the southern border of the
Tuscan marches. This is a few miles from Orbi-
tello, on the Mediterranean, and less than one hundred miles from Rome. His father was named
Bonizo, and was a carpenter, or, in the opinion of
others, a goatherd.

At his baptism the child received the German
name of Hildebrand, which was modified by the
Italian pronunciation to Hellebrand. The hostile
German punsters changed this into Höllebrand, or

Brand of Hell, while the zealous monkish adherents interpreted it as Hellbrand, a pure flame, using as a basis the many legends of supernatural signs of favor and Divine choice that were associated with his youth. The world has always known him by the simple baptismal name, Hildebrand, the greatest hero of the Roman Church. The man, in his conceptions and conduct, was greater than the office to which he came, so the final judgment of history has given the Papal title of Gregory Seventh a secondary place to the humble cognomen of his infancy. For there is no doubt of his lowly, peasant origin, and his career is a brilliant testimony of the democracy that obtained in the ecclesiastical system of Rome, whereby the lowest not infrequently came to the highest seats of honor. One of the greatest elements of strength through the centuries, reckoned next to its faith, was this opportunity given by the hierarchy to the common man for every preferment.

Innumerable stories describe the precocity of the lad, evidently pointing to the truth that he had more than usual intelligence. The advice was given to the carpenter that his son be allowed to follow letters, and in that day it meant the Church. Happily there was a maternal uncle in Rome, the abbot of the Monastery of St. Mary on the Aventine. This kinsman held the third place among the twenty assisting the Pope in the mass. Famous men came frequently to the retreat of this monastery, among them, Odilo, the saintly Abbot of Cluny, and Laurentius, the learned Bishop of Amalfi. The youth pursued the courses of the trivium and quadrivium, as then given. The teaching comprised the ready use of the Latin language, the rules of rhetoric and dialectics, the reading of the fathers and holy books, the ritual, and chanting. All this breathed the inmost spirit of the Church, and it was of vital moment for his career that he was able to study at Rome, since here all the sanctity, science, and refinement of the West converged. The authority of the Apostolic See was ever before his mind, so that later Hildebrand could say that "St. Peter has nourished me from infancy beneath his wings, and has fostered me in the lap of his clemency."

The disposition of the student was congenial to his surroundings, and he practiced the severe regulations of the Benedictines. Self-denial in the most trivial things taught him that rigor which he laid upon mankind. It was both his discipline and his pride to triumph over every indulgence of the senses. But this monastic perfection was attained at that period only in the foundation of Cluny. Thither, in Burgundy, Hildebrand went to the strictest religious house in Europe. Here his faculties were fully trained for every encounter of the future, and advanced courses taken in the arts and theology. Cluny was beautiful in location and surrounded by highly cultivated gardens. The purest, ablest minds of the times were assembled here, so

that in this congenial company the zealous neophyte
might well have decided to remain permanently.
He gave himself likewise to solitude and to medita-
tion on the condition of the Church and of society.
The depth of his devotion would possibly seem to
incline him to prefer this retreat, but he possessed
a restless desire for activity.

Plans for reformation were in his heart; but
when the program was revealed to the abbot, the
only counsel he received was, "Pray, be pure, and
hope for the best." Several years were spent at
Cluny (some have estimated between the ages of
sixteen and twenty-three). In the end he was a
thorough monk; but there is no record as to where
the novitiate was finished and the profession made,
whether at St. Mary's or Cluny. He had been
strengthened and tempered; asceticism had made
him fit in character, while, of paramount value to
his future success, the powerful monastic order of
St. Benedict was knit to him by bands of steel.
Hildebrand returned to Rome, likely on some errand
for his order. A further tradition makes him de-
ciding to leave Rome in despair of his improving
affairs, when a vision of St. Peter came to him,
calling him to return to the place of trial and
service. His former instructor, John Gratian, having become Pope Gregory VI, in 1046, the young
monk was attached to the Papal service as a chap-
lain, though he was only in sub-deacon's orders.
He also served as clerk and gave his zealous sup-

port to the program of law and order which his patron tried to establish. When the fickle populace preferred anarchy and rapine, and the Council of Sutri gave its decrees, Hildebrand gladly followed the deposed Pope to his retreat upon the Rhine, and within a few months became his heir. No place was then so inviting as Cluny, and its welcome portals received its son, whom speedily the monks elected to the office of prior. The new spirit aroused in the Church will not allow the talents and energy of this Cluniac exponent to remain remote from the heat of the contest, and his great career was soon to start.

CHAPTER II.

THE EVOLUTION OF AN INSTITUTION.

As a religion grows in social influence and obtains wide application in the lives of persons and of a nation, it is necessary to consider it as an institution. There will have arisen a ritual, a priesthood, a constitution, and a theology. The centuries of propaganda, persecution, and apology in the history of our Christianity are fundamental and formative. But the Church as it concerns the history of Europe came to be identified with the foundation of Rome.

Machinery can never dispense with actual power, while form and symbol are vain without the enduement of the Spirit. For centuries the Roman Church, with its hierarchy, stood as the embodiment and supreme guide of Christianity. In St. Augustine's "City of God," the book of consolation for the believer of the fifth century and after, the ideal society was readily identified with a centralized Catholic Church.

The ecclesiastical power and command were the result of a complex growth, and the evolution of the institution must be traced in order to comprehend its culmination under the mastery of Hildebrand. Territorial, political, doctrinal, and personal factors, all contributed to this steady, triumphant advance. After Christianity became the State religion under Constantine, the Church at Rome was free from persecution. Its bishops ranked high, but not paramount to those of Alexandria and elsewhere. The location in the Eternal City, the ancient capital of the world's civilization, contributed primarily to the alleged priestly pre-eminence. The removal of the center of the civil government of the Empire to Constantinople gave a decisive opportunity for preference and influence to the Bishop of Rome. The many traditions of political greatness and the unlimited claims of hierarchical supremacy combined to the upbuilding of this sovereign institution, the Papacy. The doctrinal moderation of Rome assisted in the winning of a wide prestige for its authority. It remained firm in its adherence to the decision of the Council of Nicæa in the Athanasian controversy, while there was division in the Church of the East.

It was liberal to those who had denied the faith under persecution, as had even Cyril, named the Pope of Carthage. It decided that the ordinance of baptism need not be administered the second time, even though the original sacrament had been given by an unworthy official. In all matters the Church of the West adopted the broad practice, and opened its doors to those who in good faith

wanted to be admitted. Here, then, was a vigorous
mother Church, with its branches throughout Italy,
and a policy of aggressive missionary expansion
into the regions beyond. Churchmen of rare courage, of conspicuous Christian service, and of bound-
less ambition made their additions also to the growing structure. The first formative leader was Leo
I, justly named the Great. His tact in shaping the
doctrinal decision at the Council of Chalcedon
against the contention of Eutychus, and his brave
opposition to Attila the Hun, when his city was in
danger of capture, fixed the primacy of Rome beyond cavil or doubt. His practice was to seize
every opportunity for asserting and enforcing the
authority of his See. Also the Emperor Valentinian
III ordered the obedience of all Churches throughout Gaul to the Pontiff. But, besides this human,
natural leadership, there was a desire for the Divine sanction of the authority of the Church of
Rome, and it was Leo I who laid the corner-stone
of the hierarchy by his emphasis of the imperative
conditions of the doctrine of the Petrine Supremacy.

The dogma that the Pope was the successor
of Peter came to be held by the faithful as of equal
validity with the Incarnation and the Resurrection.
The Pope, who was both saint and statesman,
Gregory First and likewise the Great, gave the
ideal of the perfect episcopal life. His Pontificate
came in 590, after a period of confusion and decay

in the Church. He tried in many ways to avoid his election, and, when in office, refused the title of Pope or universal bishop. By the faithfulness of his ministrations, by his comprehensive policy, by his missionary zeal, by his attention to the minute details of a vast and varied administration, by his care as a true shepherd of souls, he gave a spiritual leadership to Rome that was incomparable and invincible. These two Churchmen can scarcely be considered as thorough Popes; for, in a mediæval sense, the Holy Father must have both spiritual and secular sway. They were more of the nature of moral patriarchs. But the temporal element came to cast its shadow over the religious. Earthly ambitions were satisfied only with the possession of things of sense to be measured and handled. Gregory II, in 726, asserted first the separateness of the Church from the jurisdiction of the Empire, when Leo of Constantinople would enforce his decree against the worship of images upon the West. Gregory III reaffirmed this new independence of Rome from temporal control when he did not seek the customary Eastern confirmation of his election. Later he called upon Karl Martel for protection against the assaults of the heretical Lombards of North and Central Italy. The Franks accepted the military guardianship of the Church, and soon the donation of Pepin to Stephen, in 755, started the Papacy on its perilous career of landed proprietorship. The keys of twenty-two cities, cap-

tured from the Lombards through the Apennines
and along the Adriatic, were handed over by the
Frankish king, and the Patrimonium Petri thus
attained a local habitation.   But the Pope did not
enter into the administrative possession of this territory; it was held rather in the relation of fealty.
Next, a partnership for mutual benefit was struck
with Charlemagne, and Leo III assumed before the
world the right and the power to crown officially,
on Christmas day, the mightiest sovereign of
the new barbarian civilization.   This was a momentous reversal of the relations of Church and
State, and the fact of an emperor on his knees
before St. Peter's confession was worked into an
enduring mosaic for the gaze of the rulers and
potentates throughout the Middle Ages.   The sure
basis of the ecclesiastical and temporal supremacy
of the Church was finally laid by Nicholas First,
and likewise the Great, in his episcopacy from 858
to 867.

Apparently the higher the ground of authority
that he assumed, the more certain was acquiescence
and obedience to follow.   He was called to mediate
in the affairs of the Eastern Church, and gave his
decision as an absolute, independent high priest.
Nicholas announced to Constantinople that no appeal could be made from the authority of Rome,
that the privileges of Rome were eternal, derived
from no Council, but granted directly by God Himself.   Also this Pontiff established the sway of the

unlimited hierarchy. The independence of the
Gallican Church was broken, and the lowliest priest
became directly amenable to the Holy See, rather
than to the metropolitan bishop. The king, Charles
the Bald, brought the aid of the State to wrest from
the learned Hincmar, Archbishop of Rheims, the
power and right of discipline of suffragans. The
weakness of the Carolingian rulers gave Nicholas a free hand. The unjust divorce proposed by
King Lothaire from his faithful wife allowed the
Pope to become the authoritative, universal champion of public morality. A much-needed standard
of righteousness for the royalty was established,
and all the penalties of the Church stood ready to
enforce this laudable censorship. Nicholas also
affirmed that the grant of imperial power must be
confirmed by the authority of the Holy See, and
he sent out his legates to be the advisers of rulers.
The outlines and the spirit of these pretensions to
the supremacy of the Papacy had been foreshadowed in his predecessors, but this Pontiff by
his unequaled opportunities and his masterful
aggressiveness realized and verified such absolutism
as the Church had never hitherto attained. He
humbled royal and episcopal power alike, and left
as his heritage for mightier hands the essence
of the Papal monarchy. Territory was now ruled
in truly regal fashion; great wealth poured into the
coffers of the Church. Nicholas also inaugurated
the practice of being crowned with the tiara. Cere-

mony and ritual took on pomp and splendor, and
the Church had completed its course of appropriating the ancient imperial ideals and forms. This
period was momentous also by reason of the appearance and acceptance of certain forged documents, the Donation of Constantine and the Pseudo-
Isidorian Decretals, which have been described as
the two magic pillars of the Holy See.

The Donation of Constantine was first officially
cited at the close of the eighth century in an im-
plied exhortation to Charlemagne to make such
bequests of land and power as the first Christian
emperor was purported to have granted, when he
turned Italy over to the Church and departed to
found a capital on the Bosphorus. The "Donation"
served frequently in the future as the sole warrant
for wholesale appropriations of territory. The evil
results of such a political career were set forth
sadly by Dante in the "Inferno:"

> " Ah, Constantine, of how much ill was mother,
> Not thy conversion, but that marriage dower
> Which the first wealthy father took from thee!"

The same document granted besides to the Pope
and clergy such dignities as the emperor and the
senate possessed. The Pope was to live in the
Lateran palace, wear a diadem and a purple cloak,
carry a scepter and be attended by a retinue, while
the clergy were to ride on white horses and receive the honors given to patricians. The Pseudo-

Isidorian Decretals embraced a collection of fifty-
nine spurious rescripts and letters, ascribed to the
Popes of the first three centuries. The earliest
knowledge Europe had of them was at the middle
of the ninth century. They had, in all probability,
been prepared at Mainz, and were used in France
to advance the Church over the laity. The metropolitan strengthened his authority over the priests
by means of them, when in turn Pope Nicholas
cited the powers given in the Decretals to the utter
defeat of Hincmar the Primate. Henceforth the
vast range of control and the precedents for summary action, furnished by the fictitious Bishop of
Seville, were freely employed by the ambitious
Pontiffs, Hildebrand basing his weightiest principles upon the alleged decisions of this shadow
Papacy.

Before these title-deeds of priestly privilege had
been manufactured, the Church was not able to
cite authentic records earlier than the time of
Siricius in 384. Meanwhile the traditions of Councils and Pontiffs had come to possess equal validity
with the Gospels and the Scriptures. Hence the
irrevocable law of remote Rome, even back to the
immediate successors of St. Peter himself, was
created out of hand by the omnipotent ecclesiasticism. In closing this hitherto fatal gap in the
records, the case for the dictatorship of the Papacy
was made complete. The only justification which
those can offer who profited, unchallenged for seven

centuries by these Decretals, is that such claims of
authority had been put forth in some other form.
if haply not by the officials erroneously accredited,
and under the conditions so clearly proven by the
Magdeburg Centuriatores as anachronistic. The
clergy of the ninth century was the only class com-
petent to expose the fraud, but as the entire affair
was designed for its advantage, it kept silence.
Thus a mass of new, unknown decrees and rescripts was accepted at Rome, where all the archives
had been exclusively held in trust. Then Nicholas,
never questioning nor protesting, gave his sanction
to their promulgation with full authority. They
ordered complete immunity to the clergy against
all complaints of the laity before the Church courts.
There were defined the sanctity, the rights, and
the appeals of the priesthood. The Pontiff was the
guardian and legislator of the faith throughout the
world. The hierarchy of the priesthood furthermore supplemented with rigor the law and tradition of the Church by the ecclesiastical terrors and
religious penalties enforced against the disobedient
and recalcitrant. Anathema and excommunication are the common property of all religious sys-
tems, but the ban and the interdict were distinctive
weapons of the Papal monarchy, used with enlarging effectiveness. Excommunication was originally
expulsion, then aggressive exclusion from the en-
joyment of certain religious rites, because of some
delinquency in faith or life. This penalty came

finally to be inflicted for secular transgressions, and
was even borrowed by the prince from the Church
to increase obedience to the civil law. The received
theory of religion was that the priest had the sole
right to administer the sacraments, and these were
essential to salvation and admission into heaven.
Accordingly, here was a thunderbolt in the hands
of the Church by the fear of which all Europe was
ruled, since the destiny of each soul was vested in
the clergy. The ban went further than the punish-
ment of the one guilty party, and included any who
would have relations with him. But most terrify-
ing was the interdict, for it extended excommunication in a measure to an entire province or kingdom. All exterior exercise of religion was stopped.
Churches were closed, the bells removed from the
towers, the dead denied burial in consecrated
ground and placed in the common fields. No rites
were administered but those of the baptism of
newly born infants and the sacrament to the dying.
Marriages were performed in the churchyards, the
use of meat on every day was prohibited, and
people were forbidden to speak to each other, to
shave their beards, or care for their dress and
appearance. The penalty fell crushingly upon those
who had neither partaken of the offense nor could
have prevented it. The interdict was the latest
resort of the Church in point of time, and its application was not so frequent until public faith in
its validity had become somewhat lessened. In all

these penalties the usurpation of Divine power was received with awe and obedience. If in every instance they had been used beneficently, society would have been improved, however heavy the spiritual yoke; but employed as weapons of ecclesiastical warfare, abuses and grievous injury were inevitable.

The eight centuries and more after the kingdom of God had been revealed to men through the Son of God had witnessed in truth the small stone, cut from the mountain without hands, filling the world once known as Roman. But the organization had come to overshadow the great body of believers. Its authority, concentrated by the several agencies enumerated in this chapter, was widely though not absolutely accepted. The culmination of universal control by the Papacy in the future might be readily predicted, since the sure progress of the institution had been the evidence of an inherent vitality.

In addition to the basal religious contribution, a service of social and ethical value had been rendered. The Roman Church established a social amity of all nations by the Christian doctrine of the moral equality and responsibility of all races and peoples. The ideal of a single and indivisible humanity, and of Rome as the capital of a Christian republic, the apostolic center of the Church, came to be accepted.

Thus the Eternal City gained a new significance in its long, eventful history. That it had not per-

ished in the Teutonic attacks and was saved from
the Lombards indicated that a greater career await-
ed it. In a loftier sense than the classical capital
of the Cæsars, the metropolis of Christianity embodied a universal principle. It must be accessible
to all persons. An ideal of a sacred center, a tem-
ple of eternal peace in the midst of contending
humanity, a universal asylum of justice, equity, and
righteousness, is one of the most sublime conceptions of mankind. Even to-day the long-cherished
dream of a world's parliament, a federation of peace,
delays its fulfillment. But the practice in the Church
must and did fall far short of the theory, intrusted
for realization to human instrumentalities. Ambition, dogmatism, worldliness were fatal barriers.
As the theocracy grew less distinct and pronounced,
imperialism became the goal. Always the fortunes
of the Church were sharply molded by the character
of its presiding officer. Although no institution in
the annals of man has had so long and so mighty a
line of rulers, the vicissitudes of efficiency and integrity are bewildering and extreme. If the Pope
were a man of character and genius, his high office
made him supreme over all interests. The makers
of the Papacy, Leo I, Gregory I, Nicholas I, Hildebrand, and Innocent III, tower high as men who
would have been heroes in any age or cause.

On the other hand, the degradation of the Pontificate under vicious, ignoble Churchmen or by the
machinations of political factions seemed absolutely

irremediable. Such an era prevailed throughout
the tenth century and later when the Church in
its official organization entered into the Valley of
the Shadow of Death. The record for a period of
two hundred years was with a few exceptions
wicked and baleful. From Nicholas to Benedict IX
there were thirty-nine incumbents of the Holy See.
Of these, six were murdered, five sent into exile,
four deposed, and three resigned. Against many
more of the list, some violent, extraordinary, or
disgraceful circumstance was recorded. The corpse
of one Pope was exhumed, dressed in the Papal
habiliments, and before a Council arraigned for
trial. The dead Formosus was sentenced to have
three of his fingers cut off, to be stripped of his
vestments, and thrown into the Tiber. His Papal
judge in turn was soon strangled, and then the
successor of the faction favorable to the condemned
had a second Council, which restored all honors to
Formosus, whose remains were recovered for burial
in St. Peter's. One Pontiff entered into his infalli-
bility at twelve years of age. Another took to himself a double in authority, whose function it was to
be armed with the sword and join in bloody battle
for Rome. Finally the temporal had become so
confused with the spiritual that the son of Alberic,
consul of a transitory revived democracy, took the
title of John XII as he administered ecclesiastical
affairs, and the title of Octavian while he ruled
the city. Two-thirds of the episcopate were two

years and less in duration. Seven assumed the
tiara in a period of six years. Repeatedly two
claimed at the same time the full honors of the
Apostolic See, and once there was a trio of con-
testants, as seen at Sutri. The manner of the
election of the spiritual monarch for Christendom
was a fruitful cause of this abasement of the institution. Rome exercised the prerogative of naming
the head of the Church, and then, during the Iron
Age, showed less respect to his dignity and sanctity
than any other portion of Europe.

Italy was in a state of anarchy after the dissolu-
tion of the Frankish Empire, and Rome was in turn
ruled by adventurous soldiers, feudal counts, demo-
cratic factions, or religious combinations. These
varying constituent bodies would successively elect
the Pontiff. Caprice, crime, intrigue, or gold, again
and again, dictated the choice. It is not to be
thought strange that this supreme official should
happen to be a licentious and violent personage, or
simply a colorless figurehead. Such conditions allowed the ignoble rule of the Pornocracy, and the
bastard son, grandson, and great grandson of a
harlot sat in the chair of St. Peter. When affairs
grew intolerable, Otto the Great intervened from
Germany, and in a Council removed John XII. The
conditions, after this experiment equally deplorable,
are vividly portrayed by Arnulf, Bishop of Orleans,
in an address before a Synod in 991. He said:
"Once we received from Rome the glorious Leo

and the great Gregory. What do we see in these times? When the emperor departed, John turned back, drove out Leo, lately advanced from layman to Pope, cut off the nose, tongue, and right hand of his deacon, besides murdering many of the nobles, and then died. The Romans elected Benedict V, who in turn was sent into eternal exile by the emperor, when Leo was restored briefly. Otto II succeeded Otto I, but in Rome a terrible monster, Boniface, took the Apostolic See, yet dripping with the blood of his predecessors, and surpassed all in violence and outrage." The relapse under the domination of the Consul Crescentius led Otto III to try the plan of selecting the Pope from the Germans, and the learned, pious Gerbert, as Sylvester II, took the double keys with his program of an intellectual new birth. This recovery was temporary, and, after the rule of the reforming Benedict VIII, a violent reaction took place. Then again from this hotbed of corruption, and in the very period when the Pontiff was most despised and rejected, a new life manifested itself. The independence and the integrity of the Papacy came to be a practical truth. It would seem that nothing short of a miracle could have compassed the deliverance from such profound depths of disaster and iniquity. A greater contrast between the utter decay and the sudden recovery of the same power is nowhere else found in history. With the last half of the eleventh century, Rome became, as never before,

the pillar and the ground of truth.   The times were
ripe to cause this startling transformation and
mighty advance; but the personality of one man
was the largest element in its achievement, for Hildebrand, both by inheritance and by design, entered
his allotted place in the events of the world as the
master-builder of the Papacy.

CHAPTER III.

THE CONDITION OF THE CLERGY.

ALONG with the abasement of the Apostolic
See there existed widespread demoralization among
the clergy and a low spiritual life in the laity. However unduly the historian may have emphasized the
centuries from the ninth to the twelfth as the Dark
Ages, there was a culmination of reaction from the
ideals and teachings of earlier eras before the
close of this mediæval period. The Crusades can
not be named as the sole cause of the new tone and
vigor which marked the life of the Church and of
society. But antecedent to this quickening, the
sway of feudalism had slight alleviation. The day
of chivalry was not fully come. The serf lacked the
hope of any possible escape from his status. However, wealth was increasing and commerce was
ready for encouragement. Cities were growing in
population, upon whose masses the breath of the
new democracy of the communes would soon move.
While these germs of material progress were thus
dormant, there prevailed in the main a period of
intellectual sterility. Learning was practically confined to the Church, yet a Council, held in 992, said

that scarcely a single person was to be found in
Rome itself who knew the first elements of letters.
Very frequently the clergy could not write or trans-
late a Latin letter, and the homilies they preached
were compiled for their use by the bishops from
the writings of the Fathers. The influence of the
monasteries, while at the same time they alone preserved and housed the precious manuscripts of
learning, was actually exerted against ancient literature. Odilo, the holy abbot of Cluny, relates that
in his youth he had been seduced by the charms of
the Greek and Latin writers; but having fallen
asleep one day over his beloved Virgil, he had seen
in a dream his text change to a beautiful antique
vase, and from it there issued a brood of writhing
serpents. From that time he never again touched
his classics. Great scholars and theologians were
scarcely found for generations, and the brilliant
Gerbert was judged by his contemporaries to be a
magician.

A type of the roughness of the manners of the
times may be cited in Fulk the Black, the progenitor
of the Plantagenets, who rode his rebellious son
with spur and bit, and then, a penitent pilgrim himself, was led by a bridle through the streets of
Jerusalem. While the clergy were never more igno-
rant, neither had they been more sensual nor more
worldly than in the eleventh century. They were
rich and powerful, but exceedingly corrupt. It followed, as a natural sequence, that a lack of rectitude

and a lowering of standards in the hierarchy excused the shortcoming of the acolyte. The bishops, who should have been examples and have enforced correct living, were least qualified to employ stern measures. They were often thrust into their positions by violence or intrigue, as in the case of many elections of the Pope. A child of five years was made Archbishop of Rheims, the metropolitan authority of France; and the See of Narbonne was bought for another of the age of ten. Again, the great mass of the clergy was evilly influenced by its political and social environment. The feudal lord too frequently bent the priest to his will instead of bowing the suppliant knee to the wishes and welfare of the Church. The practice had become widespread to transform the bishops into feudal barons. The episcopate and the abbacy were more and more filled by the direction of the king or count. Through this principle of investiture exercised by the rulers, there was given control of both offices and lands. The spiritual services of the higher clergy became overshadowed by their political duties as councilors of State, ministers of princes, and governors of provinces. The helmet was now more frequently donned than the miter. It seemed that spirituality would be merged into the feudal system, and the priesthood would enjoy its rights only by secular tenure. Having the occupations of the temporal nobility, it was inevitable that the clerical chiefs assumed their manners and

habits. Dissoluteness, luxury, and unhallowed ambition prevailed with lamentable frequency. The
decay in right living by the leaders brought a loss
of influence over the thinking and beliefs of the
people. The true public demands consistent examples of piety and virtue, and in a superstitious age
expected ascetic observances, self-denial, and a rigid
regimen. These standards were proclaimed by the
monastic orders, or the regular clergy, as they were
called, in contradistinction from the secular or
ordinary clergy. Hence a superiority was accorded
by the people, who paid a deeper respect to the monk
than to the parish priest.

These two agencies of the Church were by no
means harmonious, nor had they been equally
guiltless of lapses to worldliness and sin. The
secular clergy dwelt in the world among men, occupied with the care of the spiritual concerns of their
communicants. In their function of the "cure of
souls" they administered the sacraments as being
the essence and entirety of the religious profession.
The parish was the smallest ecclesiastical territory,
and must contain at least ten families. The priest
was admitted into his sacred calling, the "holy orders," by the bishop, and his appointment to a
field of labor came from the patron of the parochial
Church with the approval of the bishop of the diocese. The patron was a person, lay or clerical, to
whom the church property belonged. The bishop
received his place, according to the canon law, by

the election of the clergy and the people. It will be seen that the term people admitted of broad construction, for it included every landholder of the neighborhood. Since this involved the immediate feudal owner, the over-lord, and the distant prince, the determining voice in the choice of the bishop was likely to be earthly.

In connection with the duties of the bishop at the cathedral, there was required a body of secular clergy to assist. This was known as the chapter, and often its interests were opposed to that of the bishop by reason of feudal privileges and connections. The members of the chapter were known as canons, and for their discipline and direction a rule was created somewhat like the organization of the Benedictines, yet not even its milder obligations were possible to be enforced without interruption.

Monasticism came out of the East, but it developed in the West to be the most efficient instrument of the Church. Its well-known vows are poverty, celibacy or chastity, and obedience. From the foundation of St. Benedict at Monte Cassino, in 529, there was a disposition to independence of control. But the capitularies of Charlemagne placed the monks under the jurisdiction of the bishop in whose diocese they lived. This law was resisted by the Benedictines, because it assigned an inferior place to the principle of asceticism upon which their system was founded. The sentiment of Europe encouraged this antagonism, since the

belief prevailed that a monk was a better man than
a priest. In spite of the nature of the monastic
obligations, the history of the order reveals a
strange contradiction. The pledge to poverty did
not prevent the brotherhood from growing very
wealthy and amassing broad acres. The obedience
of the individual monk to the command of the
abbot was merely the means whereby the authority
of the order should be made to prevail throughout
the entire social fabric. Since the monasteries held
lands in feudal tenure, there developed the covet-
ousness of the bishops and the rulers, so that Germany and France saw many struggles for their rich
possessions. But the strife of the secular and the
regular clergy included the more vital matters of
discipline and conduct, in which the monks gave
their vigorous support to the mightiest movements
of the Church. Yet before this heroic service was
rendered, the Benedictines had passed through not
one, but many periods of relapse. Gluttony and
idleness were the usual faults of the common monks,
if there was nothing less venial. Lay abbots
often gained control, and under their rule the
cloisters were given over to revelry, sports, and
vicious amusements. The cupidity, coarseness,
drunkenness, and hypocrisy of the monks were more
than matched by the excesses of the priests. However, in the case of the secular clergy it is just to
recall, that the doctrine had been evolved that the
chief part of the priestly function was to administer

the sacraments by which Divine grace was conveyed
from God to man.

Now for the efficacy of this service it was held
that the personal character of the priest was not a
matter of consideration. Such a separation of the
man from his religious office lost him a powerful
safeguard in his private integrity, and while the
Church without doubt desired an upright ministry,
there was no official action to maintain it. The
monk, on the other hand, had no possible excuse
for a fall from rectitude, since he had voluntarily
pledged himself to the strictest standard of life.
Yet his high profession seemed unattainable for
any length of time, and the story is an oft-repeated
one of deterioration and unfaithfulness. The ideals
were not forgotten, however, and there was always
courage for reform. The one remedy proclaimed
in every instance was more monasticism; the original principles must have a more thorough enforcing—just as to-day the cure for the ills of democracy
is prescribed by some politicians to be more democracy. The most notable wave of correction in
Europe went forth from the monastery of Cluny.
This new center of Church life was established by
the gift of a Duke of Aquitaine on the Saone River,
near Macon, and placed under the direct jurisdiction of the Pope. It reaffirmed the original rules
of St. Benedict, and the success of this foundation
in Burgundy caused similar movements in Italy,
Suabia, and Saxony. Monte Cassino, the birthplace

of the order, restored its discipline, and the Abbey of St. Mary on the Aventine, the future school of Hildebrand, was created by Alberic, the consul, to be the exponent at Rome of the revival. After Charlemagne, there had ensued a period of monastic expansion, the number of monks in Europe being said to have reached one hundred thousand. Now, the new feature which Cluny contributed was its supervision. The abbot of the parent society had an oversight of all the monasteries which had accepted the reformed life. His power fairly rivaled that of the Pope himself, and the number of institutions which composed the powerful "Congregation of Cluny" reached many hundreds, if not two thousand. Very soon Cluny was known as a party with a program. These monks knew the political axiom that policies are promoted and results attained through agitation and organization. Emperors enrolled themselves as partisans, and even before the crucial campaign of the later eleventh century the combination of prince, Pope, and Cluny had made a stir in the West.

The paramount service of the "Congregation" was the advocacy of the two reforms of which Hildebrand became the victorious champion. The two notorious clerical crimes, the gravest violations of ecclesiastical law, were simony and concubinage. The terrible abuse, appropriately known as "simony," accompanied the practice of investiture. The name took its origin from the New Testament narrative where the magician Simon asked the apostles for the gift of the Holy Spirit, offering to pay money in exchange for it. The condemnation by Peter on that day fixed forever the attitude of the Church to all material considerations. "Thy money perish with thee, because thou hast thought that the gift of God may be purchased with money." (Acts viii, 30.) In the accepted doctrine, the imposition of the bishop's hands was believed to impart the Holy Spirit, so that the buying and selling of ordination, the priestly function, and of admission into monastic orders, and any traffic in ecclesiastical offices, were regarded as simony. The canonical usage required the election of officials by the clergy and the people, and, in the case of abbots, by the members of the order. Sovereigns once had merely ratified the choices; but with the growth of feudalism and the right to rule over extensive territory, it became the custom to grant the honors and estates upon the condition of the payment of money. Charlemagne is said to have introduced the ceremony of placing the ring and crosier in the hands of the bishop, as symbolic of his spiritual authority, usurping this prerogative from the archbishop. The continuance of this practice by other princes fastened upon all those who ministered in holy things a subordination with infinite capacity for evil. But simony was an abuse of clerical as well as of secular patrons, for bishops and princes alike were possessed by an excessive greed. The lower offices in the Church could not be obtained without a payment to those higher in control. In modern phrase, the prevalent system would readily be catalogued as "ecclesiastical graft." The Church of Milan had the evil repute of prices fixed by its archbishop for each office of the inferior clerks.

The causes which had produced this lamentable situation were numerous and powerful. A career in the Church brought high social distinction, and great families contrived to have their sons, irrespective of their fitness, placed in the influential offices. The bishop or the abbot also enjoyed political pre-eminence. His sway of lands gave his voice weight in the Council chamber, and the German rulers devised that the Church dignitaries should be a balance against the feudal nobility. The sordid, material motive entered, in that the treasury of the prince was filled by the contributions from these lucrative positions. Feudalism was of the nature of a bargain, a *quid pro quo*, protection matched against service, and the cash, or its equivalent, was a return for the chance to be ordained. From the excuse of the Churchman, that his possessions would be used by him for pious purposes, it was a short step to where he coveted the wealth for its personal gratifications. The riches of the Church proved to be the deadly peril of its agents. Offices not being bestowed for merit or service, every degree of corruption and inefficiency was possible. Sycophants, adventurers, court buffoons, and the half-witted offspring of royalty, became lofty prelates. The evil influence upon the clergy was most appalling. Rapacity and all human passions prevailed, while avarice, luxury, and prodigality poured in like a flood. The priest lost his concern for the spiritual welfare of his flock. All things were measured by the secular standard. The religious interests of the diocese were displaced by the necessity to work for the material aggrandizement of the See, while the relations of the bishop and his subordinates tended to be chiefly commercial. The effect of simony on society was equally disastrous. The layman could say truthfully, every ecclesiastic has his price. When the Church forfeited its leadership, there was no other power left to guide men. When the guardians of the higher standards of conduct were recreant to the faith once professed, the public of Europe fell into the deeper mire of sin and worldiness.

For centuries the great Councils had sounded the alarm against simony. Popes had denounced it, and the wise Sylvester II demanded its suppression. Yet even Pontiffs continued to purchase the Holy See. It remained for the true Christian Emperor Henry III to open the warfare, when, in 1044, before an assembly of German clergy, he commanded the extermination of the practice.

The second vast reform that Cluny stood for was the celibacy of the clergy. This was an obliga-

4

tion on the monk; but the secular clergy had not accepted the standard, for they lived in formal marital relations, or possessed women and concubines. This was almost a universal custom, and Lombardy in Italy was foremost in the practice, Milan being the very center of opposition to celibacy. The German and French clergy in large part were married, and England had failed to prevent the canons from taking the same step as its parochial clergy. Even the prohibitive vow of the Benedictines had been broken; for the fiery apostle, Peter Damiani, in his book entitled "Gomorrah," exposed the nameless sensual vices that polluted the monastic life. But the pledge to chastity was the very essence of asceticism. An Oriental idea of the inalienable evil of matter had helped the prevalence of the notion that celibacy was the condition most favorable to Christian perfection. It had been the state of the foremost saints, and the worthies of the first four centuries followed the precept of St. Paul, rather than the practice of St. Peter. This ideal for the clergy was popularly approved early in the West, so that it is not strange that, in 365, the Spanish Council of Elvira passed the first order against the marriage of the clergy. This principle was formally incorporated in the Latin Church, in 385, by a decretal of Siricius. The Church of Africa accepted the ruling; but the Cisalpine division was disposed to compromise in its obedience. The law remained, forbidding any

relations with women, but, by the connivance of
the superior officers, the restrictions were not enforced. Gregory I, in 590, tried a measure of
reform, but his main efforts were to prevent a
second marriage of priests. The Bishop of Metz, in
762, gave a new impetus to the movement by increasing the control of the bishops over the lives
of canons; yet wedlock was freely resumed in the
next century. The sin, in fact, of the Popes stood in
the way of enforcing the principle. Next, a new
penalty was provided that forbade the children of
priests to be appointed to the offices of the Church.
Restrictive legislation was resumed at the Council
of Augsburg in 952, the plan now being devised
of inflicting stripes on the women. The Bishop of
Verona proposed, in 987, to debar married priests
from their functions, and the Emperor Otto agreed
to sustain the action. Such a revolt was raised
thereupon by the clergy that the prosecution was
stopped.

Henry II, called the King of the Priests, at the
Synod of Pavia, in 1022, protested against the general laxity of the times, and Benedict VIII published edicts that, unless their wives were abandoned, the married clergy would be suspended from
office. Their children were made serfs of the
Church, and the women in many instances were
whipped or banished. But the habits of long stand-
ing did not speedily change, even though both the
Papal and the imperial sentence had been pro-

nounced against concubinage. A bitter defense by the priests with families ensued against the rigorous program of the Cluny congregation. Clearly it would contribute signally to the advance of the power of the Papacy should celibacy prevail. Pontiff and monks alike were working for the absolutism of the Church. In excluding its other ministers from domestic life, their entire affection would be centered upon the religious organization. It became home, family, occupation, sustenance, the very existence, the all in all, of the man who had taken its vows. The observance of chastity separated the clerical orders from the people by an impassable barrier, and in the practice of its austerities they earned the reverence to which they laid claim.

Another concern of the Church was that its rich possessions should be preserved for it inalienably. If marriage became the accepted rule, then the property of the priest would be transmitted by descent. This practice did obtain for a time in Spain, and fathers elsewhere used many devices to make secure the future of their sons. Then, if violation of the long established but little honored rule were to occur, the dignitaries objected less to concubinage than to marriage with its rights of inheritance. As long as clerical conduct did not harmonize with the canon law, there was grave peril in store. One sin led to others more grievous. The female partners were too frequently everything that was base. When consistency was lost, all sorts of excesses followed. The frailties of the leaders of the spiritual kingdom, which have been recounted, tell the familiar story of the power of sin over the human heart.

The cause of Christ had been wounded in the house of His friends. Happily, however, there were those who ceased not to lift their voices against wickedness in high places. The vision of the pure heart, clean hands, and loyal service was ever cherished by the faithful. The despondent took inspiration again in the thought that the Christian religion had been the great moral element of the centuries. It was the one agency that had acted visibly on the lives of men. It was the natural protector of the poor, the weak and the helpless. It yet taught the reverence of women, benevolence to all classes, and personal self-denial. It constantly elevated the noblest elements of human nature in its religious, moral, and social instincts. Its influence was ever exerted to minimize the evils of feudalism. The disastrous failure of mediæval government occurred in its administration of justice. There was a widespread absence of law, and no adequate authority existed to enforce what was right and equitable. Personal justice came to prevail, and feudalism permitted private warfare to settle grievances. To stop this practice both the secular and the regular clergy of France and of Germany joined their forces. The Church directed its members to observe the "Peace of God;" that is, to refer all disputes to the civil tribunals. Failure to obey, however, could be punished only with the spiritual penalties. The tenth century was still too warlike to stop all fighting, so the clergy had to compromise in "the Truce of God." This pledged the feudal baron to keep the peace from Wednesday night until Monday morning in each week. This prohibition became more effective in the eleventh century, as its sanction changed from the Gottes-frieden to the Landesfrieden. The peace of the land was proclaimed by the king or emperor, and must be obeyed under pain of civil punishments. The Pope added his confirmation by incorporating the reign of peace in the canon law. Such a union of Pontiff, emperor, and clergy of all classses was an earnest of what the Christian sentiment of Europe could accomplish, if it set itself resolutely to correct the abuses which sapped the strength of the Church. These frailties and sins were ever a challenge to some zealous soul of dauntless faith. It remained for Hildebrand to become the peerless champion of principles hitherto advanced in weakness and falling upon the ears of those who contemptuously disregarded or wantonly disobeyed the truth.

CHAPTER IV.

THE SWAY OF THE GERMAN POPES.

In the history of the Holy Roman Empire, Mr. James Bryce gives an elaborate exposition of the theory of the Church and State in the Middle Ages. He says that the two great ideas bequeathed by an expiring antiquity were those of a World Monarchy and a World Religion. The relation of the imperial and the Papal power is explained under the emblem of body and soul. The emperor was God's Vicar in matters temporal, and the Pope, Vicar in matters spiritual. Opposition between two servants of the same king is inconceivable, and thus is created a perfect plan for the union of Church and State. But such an accord of Papal and imperial authority was impracticable and unhistoric. It may have existed in a measure under Charlemagne; then again more accurately with Otto III and Sylvester II, and possibly, having the emphasis on the imperial part, under Henry III and Leo IX. This ideal equilibrium of interests never long endured, and it was a broad sweep from the Papacy as an appanage of Germany to the extravagant profession of Boniface VII, who shouted as he grasped a scepter and a sword, "I am Cæsar, I am the Emperor!"

The history of the city of Rome is distinct from that of Italy, yet it has much of obscurity as to its internal affairs from the seventh to the eleventh centuries. Its position with that of the Church in its midst was one of political dependence. When the Exarch departed from Italy, deference continued to be paid to the Empire seated at Constantinople. The election of a Pope was reported to the East for approval. Accordingly, the choice fell most frequently on a priest of Greek descent. Doctrinal differences in the iconoclastic contest encouraged the West to the repudiation of political control. But the appeal to the Franks for aid against the Lombards by the Church was once more a recognition of the superiority of the State. It was to the material gain of the Papacy to have the imperial idea revived, and the assumption of the right to confer the title of emperor upon Charlemagne and his successors became the most valuable asset of the hierarchy. This mighty Carling was, when occasion demanded, the master in civil and doctrinal affairs, but at Rome his *missi dominici* were alone the casual signs of his authority. Under Lothaire the noted constitution was issued which provided that there should be no election to the Holy See without the consent of the emperor. The traditions of power were not lost, and the republican atmosphere encouraged self initiative. When the Franks failed to aid against the Arab assaults, Leo IV rallied the resources of the city and decisively repulsed the invasion. In the decay of the dynasty, the Church selected the kings whom it would crown emperor, thus bringing the Empire to nothingness by the end of the ninth century. Then ensued a fictitious independence of the city that was marked by the gravest disorders. The titles of a once potent consul, tribune, or senator appear in the civil list, but the Church had fallen into the grasp of local factions, and was an institution without secular influence.

When Otto the Great brought Rome back to its subordinate place in the revived Empire, his intervention was accepted with bad grace. By the notable Constitution of Otto, in 962, the clergy once more made covenant that no election to the Pontificate should be completed until the sovereign of Germany had given approval. This relation was actively construed to mean the removal of an unworthy incumbent. Otto used his power cruelly, and was a tyrant to both Church and populace. The coronation at St. Peter's, however, restored the European prestige of the Papacy, and the feeling grew that led men to look on the Holy See as the legitimate granter of all thrones. Each Cisalpine ruler pursued the will-o'-the-wisp of Roman favor, since it came to be an accepted fact that the king of the Germans could not enter into the title of emperor until he was crowned by the Pope. Force of arms frequently was required to compel the coveted ceremony, so that the antipathies of Roman and German grew more violent with the succession of ambitious Northern invaders. The advent of Henry II was marked by the burning of Pavia; but Conrad II fixed his mastery more securely in Northern and Central Italy by establishing the feudal code and tenure. The Church was regarded as a secular body by him, and offices were given in exchange for political services. The classification of the clergy was fashioned already like to the feudal form, and this new impetus threatened to make the conditions the same as those of a mere human organization. Under Henry III the bondage of the Church to the dictates of the State was made complete in the choice of its episcopacy. He appointed the bishops of Germany and Italy freely. To be sure, he desired worthy candidates. They must be canonically fit, as to rank and service. The emperor was hostile to simony so far as it included the actual use of money. At a Council in Germany he took oath, "As God has freely of His mere mercy bestowed upon me the crown of the Empire, so will I give freely and without price all things that pertain to His religion." But he held firmly to his right of investiture, and his policy was strengthened by the climax of power he attained in the length and breadth of his domain. From the imperialistic view-point, the notion having currency that the Church was intrusted to the State, it was natural that Henry III entered his career of dictator of the Apostolic See. The abject surrender of the right of nomination by the Council was a sad confession of the complete abandonment at Rome. Since no worthy material was to be found there, the emperor turned to the North. In three hundred years, only two persons who were not Italians had worn the tiara. Four German Pontiffs in succession were now sent to the South. Clement II, whose elevation occurred after the momentous Council at Sutri, did not complete his first year. After an interval, Poppo, Bishop of Brixen, was selected and taken by the Margrave of Tuscany to Rome, were he assumed the name of Damasus II. Within twenty-three days he had passed away, whether by the Italian fever or Italian poison, accounts differ. The climate was a strong fortress to Italy through the ages, and had put to flight, if not to death, many a military and secular invader. Now it seemed arrayed against the clerical intrusion. There was, accordingly, a well-founded aversion among the German prelates to accept the fatal honor. But the Roman clergy resignedly asked the emperor for a third leader, and a great Council at Worms considered the request. The lot fell on Bruno, Bishop of Toul, a relative of the royal family. This was an illustrious personage. He was of attractive appearance, an able preacher, and accomplished in the sciences, especially music. He had held humble positions in the Church, and was

widely famed for his extraordinary piety. He had
received a valuable training in diplomacy, for he
served with credit as an ambassador to France. His
disinclination to become Pontiff appears genuine.
Only after three days fasting and prayer and many
protestations of his unworthiness, the chroniclers
declare, was Bruno willing to assume the supreme
responsibilities. Yet this acceptance is said to have
had a condition. When and how it was named is
uncertain. It may have been a compact with Henry
III. Bruno evidently came into contact with Hildebrand at once. One account is that the monk
appeared in Worms, bearing a message from the
new Abbot Hugh, successor of the pious Odilo.
Another version is that Bruno, en route south,
turned aside at Besançon to visit the monastery of
Cluny. An invitation was given Hildebrand to be
of the entourage to Rome, and his refusal was based
on the fact that the Bishop of Toul had not been
canonically chosen. The Latin biographer of Hildebrand narrates that Bruno was exhorted to accept
the high office only at the hands of the Roman
clergy and people. He was told that God was
waiting for him to take the first step, not merely
to reform, but to recreate the Church. At any rate,
when Bruno appeared in Italy, he advanced by slow
stages in the coarse garb of a penitent, with bare
feet, leaning upon a staff and bearing the wallet of
a beggar. Multitudes attended him in the cities,
and a profound impression went abroad as he ap-

proached the sacred city, a pilgrim and not a
Pontiff. When his proviso became known, the decree of election was passed joyfully, and on February 12, 1046, the sway of Leo IX began. The
appeal to the former practice of the Church gave
the German Pope an immense initial popularity.
In the past he had been jealous in the assertion of
the rights of his bishopric and order. In the new
exalted office would he be a Churchman or an im-
perialist? He became one of the strong makers of
the Papacy. His activities were wide and hitherto
unparalleled. He abounded in resource and inven-
tion. His Pontificate brought a restoration of the
dignity and influence enjoyed by the Holy See two
centuries earlier. Leo IX contributed potently to
the spirit of reform that had begun to make some
stir.

The program that he followed may readily
be called Hildebrandine. But the claim that the
monk of Cluny was the entire inspiration of his
career seems too extreme. Hildebrand did accom-
pany him to Rome, and his presence was to be of
more value than the royal favor of princes. It
was an interval of twenty-five years before the monk
entered the succession of St. Peter; but his genius
found signal expression and employment from the
beginning. He was appointed sub-deacon and
almoner of the Pope. The Church was in a condition of abject poverty. The sacred edifices had
been stripped of their furnishings and ornaments;

the productive property at Rome seized by the
barons. Material succor was first needed, and the
practical talents of Hildebrand secured rich gifts
from the nobles of Benevento. Loans were obtained from communicants, and the friendship of
influential leaders was so cultivated that the powerful Tusculum counts did not interfere with the
restoration of economic independence.

Another field for the ability of the capable reformer opened in the directorship of the Convent
of St. Paul Fuori le Muri. This position as superior gave a thorough test of his rare administrative powers, and the results were in miniature what
he desired to bring to pass in the entire ecclesiastical
body. The monastery possessed the common faults
of the period. The discipline was neglected, women
were freely employed in the refectory, the holy
precincts desecrated by cattle, and the revenues
appropriated by the adjacent seigneurs. All these
delinquencies were rigorously corrected. The strict-
ness of Cluny prevailed in the cloister. Under the
new superior's rule, that strange ascendency which
his career shows him to have exercised over the
minds of men displayed itself in many instances.

This reform, wrought at the very gates of Rome,
was typical of the propaganda which Leo IX
directed. His conception of the Papal institution
was a universal one. He believed he had a mission
through all Western Christendom. He must do
more than sit in final judgment upon complaints

brought to him. Rather, he was to go abroad as an aggressive force to smite the sin of the unfaithful, and to make straight the paths which ran crooked in every nation. Within a month of his installation, as soon as a measure of authority and regularity was secured at the capital, the Pontiff began an extensive campaign of episcopal visitation. Four journeys were made to Germany in the course of his five years.

Near the end of the first year of Leo IX, his chief ministration to Germany occurred in the Synod at Mainz. Henry III gave the sanction of his presence, and the highest prelates attended. The Leonine program of ecclesiastical reform was published. Severe laws were recorded against simony, and certain bishops were required to take oath as to their freedom from the taint of the bargain and sale of churchly honors. The German clergy supported for the present with pride and loyalty this representative of their nation. But a sharp issue was not taken with many reprehensible practices, nor did the Pontiff press with undue rigor against his countrymen. Later the onward sweep of Papal power and its inevitable hostility to secular dictation developed an aggressive anti-Roman party to resist Leo on his subsequent missions. However, the sensational and revolutionary visit of this tour was made to France. In the past the national Church had boasted of its Gallican liberty, and now it was in arms at once against this new conception of

Papal duty. The king discouraged by correspondence the inspection, and then absented himself from
Rheims with the majority of his clergy. But the
Pope had the pretext that he was to engage in the
consecration of the cathedral which received the
remains of St. Remi, the popular saint of France,
who had baptized Clovis, the first king. Great
throngs from all quarters witnessed the ceremonies,
and the occasion was most auspicious for the intro-
duction of Leo IX to the people in the character
of intense devotion to the canonized. The conclave
which followed was a heart-searching time. The
subjects before it were simony, the apostasy of
monks, irregular divorces, the unworthy pursuits
of the clergy, the plunder of the poor, and heresy.
The character of the dignitaries was passed upon
in a similar fashion to the practice of a Methodist
Conference with its ministers. Every prelate, under
pain of anathema, was adjured to confess publicly
his sin, if he was touched by the guilt of simony.
An example was made of no less a personage than
the chief Churchman of France, Guido of Rheims.
He was charged with various grave offenses, and
after three citations he was unable to take the oath
of innocency. Bishop Hugo of Langres fled rather
than face investigation. Others were found guilty
of simony practiced in their behalf by friends. The
Pope spoke in condemnation of the prelates who,
with the king, had not attended the Synod. They
were summoned to Rome for judgment. Standards

were set up, and decrees entered against various abuses, which are strangely like those known to modern times in Catholic countries, where there has been little supervision of the priesthood. Bishops must be elected by the clergy and the people; the priests must not exact fees for burial, baptism, and visitation of the sick, and must refrain from usury and bearing arms. The celibacy of the clergy was not urged at this time, though Leo was actively supported in his reforms by the monastic foundations and the common people. He issued his commands as absolute sovereign of the Church, and took no account of the will of the king. The hostile clergy was unable to make a sustained resistance, and, however unwelcome the active participation of Rome in French affairs, its decrees were respected, and the condemned made the confessions necessary for their restoration.

When the resolute Pontiff returned to Italy, the authority of the Papacy had been immensely enhanced. His appeal to the religious reverence of Christendom awakened a new sense of the power of the Church. He furthermore laid the foundations for the popularity of the Holy See with the masses, which found increasing expression a century later, when democracy leagued with the Church authorities against imperialism. There remained, nevertheless, for the Roman institution locally a complexity of political and religious conditions to be adjusted. An enlarged plan of reform was given at the Synod in the city to which Northern and Italian prelates came. The marriage of the clergy was sternly forbidden, and women who henceforth held the position of concubines were to be sold as slaves. The clergy of Rome were ordered to leave their private houses, and occupy dwellings in common under a rigid supervision. Leo IX was actively assisted in his corrective program by Hildebrand, Hugh of Cluny, and Peter Damiani. But clerical scandals were not removed. The administration of the Church could not follow a persevering scheme of reform. Its dominion through the hierarchy was not sufficiently established. The evils were strongly intrenched. Passionate opposition began to brew on account of the new strength of the Pope. The German nominees of the emperor held many bishoprics in Italy and their disposition to assert independence of Rome aroused the antagonism of the Primate. Upon the occasion of his visits to Germany he showed himself not subservient to the desires of the imperial clergy, and humiliations were put upon him. When Leo IX essayed the part of mediator between Henry III and Hungary, neither would listen to him, and his office seemed to be without political weight.

Meanwhile the enlarging influence of Hildebrand in the religious world appeared in connection with one of the first heresy trials of the Middle Ages. Already the sub-deacon had been made a cardinal, and was given charge of the offerings

when the Pope was absent on tours. At the Synod
in Rome, Berenger, an Archdeacon of Tours, had
been condemned on the contents of a letter sent
to Lanfranc. His doctrine was copied after the
belief of Erigena of the ninth century, who had
denied the real presence of Christ in the Eucharist.
This was a reaction from the extreme utterance of
Radbertus on transubstantiation, and the re-echo of
Berenger affirmed that the mystery of the Holy
Sacrament was a symbol. This teaching was widely
promulgated in France. Berenger paid no attention
to his excommunication, and was powerfully defended, even the king being kindly disposed. When
the assault on the heretic became equally violent,
Hildebrand went to Tours to quell the feud. But
the usually stern monk on this occasion resorted
to conciliation, and persuaded Berenger to sign a
vague declaration of his belief in the changed nature
of the sacred elements. Hildebrand was said to
have promised Berenger to defend him, if he came
to Rome, and not a few believed the judge was in
sympathy with the doctrine condemned.

Leo IX had one more plan which made for an
aggressive Papacy. He wished to be a secular
prince in Italy. This desire was of signal import
to subsequent Papal history. By trade with the
emperor for the German possessions of the See
he secured rights over Benevento. This had been
held by the invading Normans, but in a brief revolt
it acknowledged the control of Rome, then lapsed

again to the foreigner. The ambition of Leo IX now brought to pass one of the startling anomalies of the Roman Church. Behold the avowed representative of God resorting to war. The mildest of men figures as a martial Pontiff. In his early career he had some experience on the field of battle, but in this conflict military sagacity was lacking, a feeble support given by imperial troops, and the main reliance placed upon rabble soldiery. The Normans were first excommunicated, and told they must leave Italy. They had entered at the first of the eleventh century as pilgrims; then they had assisted in the defense of the Greek cities against the Arabs. They were desperate fighters, and had come to hold the most of South Italy. Their power was a menace, not only to Rome, but Germany itself. Hildebrand is said by some to have encouraged Leo IX to dispute their advance. Peter Damiani strenuously advised against such a course. The issue of the one battle was speedy, and the Pontiff of Christendom fell a prisoner into the hands of his unregenerate enemies. Strangely now in turn the victorious Normans became suppliants before the Pope, craved his forgiveness, and were restored to the fellowship of the Church. These rough warriors were skilled in craft as well as valor, and it served their purpose well more than once to be the defenders of the faith. Leo IX was taken to the Benevento he had coveted, as a nominal prisoner. His humiliation over his defeat was intense, and he gave himself to extreme self-denial. Much of the day and night was spent in prayer. His couch was a mat on the ground, and his pillow a stone. Yet he ruled Europe widely from his prison, conducting an authoritative correspondence. But his austerities wore him out, and the Normans escorted him to Rome after a period of nine months. He prepared for his immediate death with a detail both weird and sublime. His coffin was placed in St. Peter's by the side of his couch, while the choir of the church was hung in black and lighted by a thousand funeral tapers. An impressive death-scene followed. He gave fervent injunctions to his attendants, and exhorted the clergy against the greatest to him of sins, simony. In the final moment the vicissitudes of his career were uppermost in mind, as he said, "The cell which was my dwelling as a monk expanded into the spacious palace of the Lateran; now it shrinks again to this narrow coffin." In the presence of a great congregation of awed and reverent worshipers, at daybreak before the altar of St. Peter's, Leo IX passed away. His purity and gentleness of personal life were ample warrant of his admittance to the calendar of saints, while his official career had demonstrated clearly that the Papacy could not be a mere appanage of the Empire. Henry III had performed a real service in rescuing the Church from local hands, but the revival of its universal character by Leo IX fixed its authority above the confines of any one nation.

The height of the influence attained by Hildebrand under this German Primacy was evidenced by the mention of him as a successor. Benizo, a partisan biographer, claims that he resisted the high office only by tears and supplications.

Now the practical politics of Hildebrand had its first conspicuous application. He knew that the Church was not sufficiently strong in Italy. There was a great latent force possible of development in time; but the support of Germany yet remained indispensable to the political existence of the Roman institution. This was not the season to make a contest for the freedom of Papal elections, nor had the evils among the clergy been appreciably abated. Accordingly, the humble sub-deacon was the head of an embassy sent to Henry III to ask the nomination of a Northern prelate. The negotiations were protracted almost a year, but the shrewdness of Hildebrand prevailed when he secured the Churchman of the royal family who had been the closest imperial adviser. Gebhart, Bishop of Eichstadt, in Bavaria, had opposed the plans of Leo IX, and worked against the hierarchical aggrandizement. The emperor was most loath to lose his counselor, but Hildebrand was insistent. A change of attitude must come with the assumption of power, when the Church rose superior to country, and the priest predominated over the individual. Gebhart accordingly was consecrated at Rome as Victor II, in 1055. The emperor soon joined him, for a

great peril confronted Germany in the affairs of
Tuscany. Godfrey, once Duke of Lorraine, the
exile, had married Beatrice, the widow of Boniface
of Tuscany, the wealthiest and mightiest noble of
Italy. His brother, Frederick of Lorraine, had been
made a cardinal by Leo IX in defiance of German
opposition, and was sent on an embassy to Constantinople. The emperor, with a strong army, hunted
down once more his former antagonist, drove Godfrey from Italy, Frederick into a retreat, and carried
Beatrice, with her young daughter Matilda, the
famous countess to be, to the North as hostages.
These masterful, brilliant women were never to
forgive the imperial power for this insult, and they
will contribute infinitely to its future humiliation.
When insurrection at home made the presence of
Henry III imperative there, no counsel was so
valued as that of Victor II in person, but in the
midst of civil conflict the great ruler died. Victor
II was left as the adviser of his son, Henry IV,
aged six, and took the double function of emperor
and Pope. His policy was one of conciliation.
Godfrey was permitted to return to Tuscany and
his wife. Frederick of Lorraine was guided into
the abbacy of Monte Cassino, the richest and most
illustrious of the Italian monasteries. In the Council
the Pope took a firm stand against simony, and
prohibited the holding of Church lands as fiefs by
the lay nobility. Hildebrand, continued in the office
of sub-deacon, appeared at times as the Papal ad-

viser. However, Victor II may not have forgiven
him for his pertinacity in urging him to the Holy
See. Then, while political matters were uppermost
in the Empire, Hildebrand was dispatched to
France for the strenuous task of reforming its
clergy. His success partook of the supernatural;
for so searching was the nature of his investigations
that the French believed that he could read the
secrets of their hearts and see the hidden presence
of the tempter.

Forty-five bishops and twenty-seven other dignitaries were said to have been constrained to accuse
themselves and resign their benefices. Victor II was
planning to hold a National Council at Rheims
when, in less than a year after his imperial master,
he died at Florence. This German Pontiff likewise
had felt the effect of the traditions of his office.
He began to assume an independent, loftier tone,
and spoke of the throne of Peter raised high above
all people and realms. Damiani had written to
Victor II, when he became tutor of Henry IV, and,
impersonating Christ, said: "I have constituted thee
Father of the emperor; I have given into thy hands
the keys of my Universal Church; and, if this be
too little, thou mayst add Monarchy to it, so that,
kings being removed, I promise thee the rights of
the whole vacant Empire." Such teaching in the
Church bore fruit in practice. Already it was true
that no Pope could be a Ghibelline.

CHAPTER V.

THE CORNER-STONE OF PAPAL FREE-DOM.

HILDEBRAND was placed in nomination for the vacant Apostolic See. He, yet a sub-deacon, was named along with four others, and they bishops, by Frederick, Abbot of Monte Cassino. But this popular and powerful Churchman was simply delaying the honor that the clergy and nobles of Rome had designed for him. The house of Lorraine, with Godfrey as the master of Tuscany and with Frederick possessing an ecclesiastical ambition as lofty as his patrician ancestry, presented a new rallying ground in Italy, a political buffer to the enlarged influence of Germany. Hildebrand was absent in Florence with the dead Victor II; but his friends at the place of decision knew his wishes. Frederick was opportunely in Rome, not yet having entered formally upon his duties at the monastery. After a day and a night of deliberation, the Lorrainer was taken, willing or unwilling, to St. Peter's by the multitude, and consecrated, under the name of Stephen IX, to the office made vacant forty days previous. The temper of the new Pope had been clearly indicated on the occasion of a mission to Constantinople. By his expression then as the legate of Leo IX, he was known to have the most absolute view of the Roman supremacy. He had been violent and intolerant in his condemnation of the creed and the ritual of the Eastern Church. He was a rigid monk, yet at the same time he had the aims of a secular prince, and was ready to advance the interests of his brother, even possibly to make him emperor. The two men who were called to the intimate support of his Pontificate were Peter Damiani and Hildebrand.

Damiani, next to Hildebrand, was the greatest reformer of the age. From a swineherd he passed to be a monk of St. Benedict, and grew strongly versed in all Christian and classic literature. His zeal was even more intense than his learning. He was in Italy the quintessence of the Cluniac ideas, and plied a cutting lash upon every wickedness of the day. He was Abbot of Fonte Avellana in Umbria, his foster convent, and Stephen made him a cardinal and Bishop of Ostia. His monastic reform was more sweeping than the liberal rule of Benedict. He increased the use of penance, and, by his insistence upon scourging, he may be considered the father of the Flagellants. Damiani was a keen observer of every form of Church activity, quick and positive in his judgments, writing voluminously and pungently. Associated with Hildebrand as his comrade, the campaign of reform which

would have ensued must have been relentless and
widespread. But first Hildebrand had to be sent
to Germany to see the Empress Agnes, to explain
the hasty election of the Pontiff and secure the
imperial approval. The widow of Henry III held
a difficult position in the midst of the feudal princes
of her land. She had a mother's jealousy for her
young son, and distrusted all who might gain an
ascendency over him. Her confidence was given
to the spiritual advisers only, and to the Church.
So that, notwithstanding the anger aroused at the
court by the Roman election, the skillful ambassador
was able to satisfy the empress of its necessity. Likewise the negotiations developed into a personal
influence by the great monk, in the name of the
Church, which should later lead Agnes to desert
her own country for a retreat in the South. In
the meantime Stephen IX was not permitted to
make any progress in his ambitious career. He had
entertained a fixed purpose against simony, which
was now attacked by his former associate, Hum-
bert, Bishop of St. Rufina. This cardinal-bishop
wrote a treatise against the prevalent evil, in which
he suggested a remedy that is a startling forecast
of the mighty issue Hildebrand was to raise. Hum-
bert asserted that investiture in Church offices by
the laity was the chief source of the clerical sin,
and the imperial power was to blame.

Stephen IX also had occasion to intervene in
the disturbances at Milan over the marriage of its

clergy. This city of Lombardy was most tenacious of its traditions. It worshiped its St. Ambrose of the fourth century as of equal reverence with St. Peter. From him its priests claimed the right of marriage, and their greatest archbishop of the eleventh century, Aribo, lived in open wedlock. But Ariald, a member of the populace, led a crusade against the practice and was the head of the "Pataria" or "party of the ragamuffins," derisively named, which, however, had the support of the monks. When he had caused a riot by his harangues and violence against the married and aristocratic clergy, a legation was sent from Rome, composed of Hildebrand, Anselm, Bishop of Lucca, later to be a Pope, and this rioter Ariald. But the three, all of the same mind, were unable to restore peace in Milan. The aggressive faction of the Pataria was no mean factor to be counted for Hildebrand in his future reform.

A visit paid by the Pope to Florence, as in the case of his predecessor, proved fatal, it being only the eighth month of his Primacy. There were the customary rumors of poison. The story was told that Stephen had given orders to the clergy and nobles, in case of his end, to nominate no successor, under penalty of anathema, until Hildebrand returned from Germany. But no longer could the customary separation into factions be postponed. When Stephen was chosen, the local Roman party, the Tuscan support, and the Papal reforming clergy, the associates of Hildebrand, had all been favorable to him.

Now the counts of Tusculum and the descendants of the once powerful Crescentius regained the ascendency in the city, and placed in the Pontiff's office John Mincius, Bishop of Velletri, one of those suggested as a candidate by the late Pope before his elevation. Personally the bishop was a worthy man, but in the higher position he would be powerless in the hands of a turbulent laity. Peter Damiani, as Metropolitan Bishop, refused to consecrate him, and another was forced to perform the ceremony, at which the name of Benedict X was assumed. The majority of the ecclesiastics fled the city. The treasures of the Church were turned over to the new masters, and the conditions existing before the era of the German Popes had returned. The news of the seizure of power by the Roman party came to Germany, whither Hildebrand had gone on one of his frequent missions. Again his political strategy gave him the place of dictator of the issue. From the empress he received the right to hold a new election, and he assembled his friends and the anti-Roman forces at Florence, where they chose Gerard, its archbishop, who became Nicholas II. This selection was particularly acceptable to Marquis Godfrey, whose troops conducted him to Rome. A halt was made at Sutri, and once again a Pope was declared excommunicated and deposed, though absent from his trial, the Vicar of the Em-

pire in Italy, the ruler of Tuscany, and Hildebrand
pronouncing the sentence. The Roman populace
turned to civil conflict before the troops of Godfrey
reached the city walls. One faction opened the
gates, the gold of Hildebrand being charged as an
agency, and, upon the successful assault of the
Lateran, the nobles retired with their booty. Benedict X fled, only to be captured later, and condemned
with bitter accusations to an imprisonment which
lasted twenty years. Hildebrand was plainly the
master of the situation, while Godfrey and Beatrice
furnished the secular support which Germany had
given in recent times. In the nation north of the
Alps, a regency that would continue several years
gave an opportune chance for changing political
alliances, and the physical force and resources
seemed now immediately at hand in Italy, which
would establish the hierarchy at Rome on a secure
basis. Nicholas II was a native of Burgundy and
had been educated with the late Pope Stephen. His
official period, though brief like that of his predecessor, bore results of largest value. His era
brought the most signal advance in the hierarchy
of Rome since the early centuries. Three months
after his ordination there was held on April 13,
1059, the revolutionary Lateran Council, meeting
in the Church of St. John Lateran.

The gathering was large, one hundred and
thirteen bishops being present, though three-fourths
of them were Italian and none German. An eccle-

siastical constitution was drafted then, which has endured to the present day. As a piece of constructive legislation it antedates the noted civil documents of England and the Continent. The authorship has been freely assigned to Hildebrand, who was without doubt the chief counselor of Nicholas II. The creation of the College of Cardinals was achieved by reason of the disasters of the past and the necessities of the future. When this method of the election of the head of the Church was definitely prescribed in a written constitution, the corner-stone of Papal freedom had been laid. Popular assemblies at Rome, as derived from the simple religious meetings of the early Christians, had long since proved to be a recreant and even a vicious agency for the selection of the Pontiff. With the interference of barons and the intrigues of unscrupulous clergy, the body was very frequently similar to a modern packed political convention. The decree of the Lateran Synod was, that after the death of a Pope the cardinal-bishops should first meet and name a successor; then the cardinal clergy of lower rank should be summoned to vote on the nominee. A new significance was given to the function of cardinal by this legislation. Hitherto the name was a title, prefixed to the order to which the person belonged, as cardinal bishop, cardinal presbyter, or cardinal deacon, and meant that these principal clergy had been called to an advisory relation to the Roman diocese. The car-

dinals had not been an organized body of any definite number before 1059, but when they were
resolved into an electoral college, an authority and
rank were given lower only than the Primacy itself.
The roster of ecclesiastics in Rome at this period
included seven cardinal bishops, those of Ostia,
Porto, St. Rufina, Albano, Sabina, Tusculum, and
Palæstrina. There were twenty-eight cardinal pres-
byters, assigned seven each to the Churches of St.
Peter's, Maria Maggiore, St. Paul, and St. Law-
rence, outside the walls. Provision was also made
for referring the choice made by the cardinals to
the people, and this practice was observed as a
matter of form for many years. The plan for the
participation of the emperor was vague. His relation to Rome was not entirely forgotten; but the
right to confirm the nomination of the college
appeared more like a personal privilege, and was
to be given as a return for the Pope's service on
crowning the monarch of the Holy Roman Empire.
The possibilities of mob-rule even yet in the Capital
City were recognized, just as France has experi-
enced to its sorrow in later centuries, and there was
a provision that the election could be held outside
of Rome and by a majority of the cardinals.

The decree was signed first by Hildebrand
under the simple title of monk, which seems a foil
to the prominent share he had in the draft. The
names of seventy-six bishops follow, and those of
many priests and deacons. When the decree was

sent to Germany, the cardinal who bore it was denied an audience, and the Empire refused to acknowledge its validity.

The College of Cardinals became, says the historian Mignet, the senate of the new Rome. It was a seeming change from a democracy to a close corporation. Yet the principle of popular election had been so grossly abused, and was so entangled with local conditions, that nothing but a radical remedy, even a departure from the spirit of the institution, promised to be a permanent correction. The adherents of the Papacy defend this severe restriction of the suffrage on the ground that the authority became lodged in an aristocracy of merit, and not of birth, to which the humblest could and did attain. It was expressly declared in the statute that the election was not to be confined to Churchmen of the city of Rome. The new order could not be invariably observed from the start. It was all-important that a rule and standard had been prescribed. In the history of nations, lapses frequently occur from the defined method of government. The Magna Charta was not always obeyed in England, yet it has been ever the national guide.

A century passed before the Papal electoral process was entirely accepted, but the maintenance of the principle gave an immediate strength to the hierarchy. Any one chosen in another fashion was uncanonical and became anti-Pope, an argument which the reform clergy urged relentlessly against

6

all its rivals. There was the possibility of the college itself, as a small body, being controlled by designing interests; but in such event the reform to be effected was individual rather than that of a method. This same Lateran Council condemned the heresy of Berenger, whose practice was to renounce his opposition to the doctrine of transubstantiation when he was brought to trial, then straightway resume his antagonism to it.

Regulations were also made for the more strict control of the canons of the Churches in their vows and living. Decrees were passed against the chronic evils, simony and the marriage of the clergy. The Lombard priests would not publish these ordinances in their parishes, for the Milanese had excommunicated the advocates of celibacy. Accordingly, Nicholas II sent an uncompromising commission, consisting of Anselm, Bishop of Lucca, and Peter Damiani, to bring the city into harmony with the oft declared principles of the general Church. Anselm had been the resolute opponent, outside of Milan, of clerical marriage. His first Papal mission to suppress it was a failure; but now, associated with Peter Damiani, the visit met with a show of success. The fierce monk from Rome was not daunted by the threats of the populace, though he was in real peril of his life. He asserted with vehemence and power the authority and Primacy of St. Peter over St. Ambrose. The archbishop was so impressed that he took a stand against simony and concubinage. Penance was to be visited upon the guilty. But the resentment aroused in the masses on account of the ecclesiastical superiority asserted by Rome repressed their zeal for reform. Milan remained then unaffected, alert to resent any change from its established practices, a center of irreconcilable hostility to the advancing reform party in the Church. There was a consistent effort under Nicholas to enforce throughout Europe the corrective principles. France gave a nominal adherence to the program, but its king at the same time insisted upon the headship of the Gallican Church. In England the commands of the Pope were received with reverence; but the German clergy broke entirely with Rome, and in a Synod declared Nicholas deposed, ordering his name to be omitted from the public prayers. Conditions were shaping towards a crisis which boded ruin to the new spirit in the Papacy, when Nicholas II perfected an alliance that made secure the epoch which had been entered, and yielded vital consequences to the career of Hildebrand. An agreement of mutual interest, something like that of Charlemagne and Leo III, was entered into by the Pope and the Normans. They had been left under the anathema of Leo IX, whom they had captured in war and returned for a ransom. Their fortunes now were directed by a new leader, Robert Guiscard, or "Slyboots," from whom the kings of Sicily sprang. The Normans had wrested from the Greeks, the Lombards, and the Saracens increasing portions of South Italy, and they wished their possessions to have an additional element of legitimacy. The Church, whether by applying a broadcast interpretation of the Donation of Constantine as to Italian soil, or through some other unexplained claim of suzerainty, was ready for such an occasion. Nicholas was invited to Melfi in Apulia, where with the feudal ceremony he invested Robert and his associates with their lands. They took oath that in confirmation of the gift of the lands, and in recognition of the obligation of fidelity, they would pay annual tribute to Rome. They also covenanted to aid with all their might the Holy Roman Church to hold the possessions of St. Peter, and to preserve the Papal office and the government. They also pledged themselves to support the new method of the election of Popes by the College of Cardinals. The Church in this proceeding borrowed directly from the political society of the age. It was its first large application of feudal control over civil rulers; but claims for such an allegiance became frequently advanced by Hildebrand and his successors. There was also an ecclesiastical purpose served in the visit of Nicholas. The Churches of the Normans were placed under the authority of Rome, and a Synod met to launch the orders against the concubinage of the priests.

In view of the uncertainty of Tuscan diplomacy and of the resentment of the former German masters, a mighty bulwark had been found for the

hierarchy in the South. An immediate test was
made of its efficacy. The actual civil power of the
Pope about the city was most feeble. The barons,
who had championed the deposed Benedict X, made
it their business to plunder the pilgrims en route
to St. Peter's and hold them for ransom. Distinguished Churchmen from England and elsewhere
were seized. Against such rapine the Normans
were appropriately employed. Set a robber to catch
a robber. They wasted their lands, and destroyed
the castles of some of the worst brigands. It is a
noteworthy fact that these counts of the Roman
party became forthwith the zealous advocates of
the interests of Germany. But acts of violence did
not cease. The city itself was largely occupied by
the fortifications of the petty nobles, who lived
defiant of restraint. The populace was turbulent
and knew no allegiance except to the highest bidder.
Amid such elements, the religious organization held
its course and planned for a dawn of better things.
Hildebrand had become archdeacon of the Roman
Church. His hand was seen in the compact with
the Normans, and, in all relations of Rome with
bishops and kings, his counsels were the guide.
An illustration may be cited in the letter which
was sent in the name of Nicholas to the Archbishop
of Rheims.

He was told, "The Apostolic See expects you
to reprove and entreat Henry, King of France, so
that he be not corrupted by the counsels of the

wicked, who think, under favor of our discords, to elude the censure apostolic; and let him beware of resisting the sacred canons, or rather St. Peter, and of thus stirring us up against him, who desire to love him as the apple of our eye." The conclusion of the writing was that "Our very dear brethren, the cardinal bishops salute you, and so does, with humility, our son Hildebrand." The spiritual son he was, indeed, of the Pope, yet not ready to enter into the heritage; for after two years of a Pontificate brief, but fraught with weighty consequences, Nicholas closed his life, July 27, 1061, at Florence. Most of the duties of the Primacy at the last had been resigned to Hildebrand, while he busied himself with deeds of charity. Now had arrived the time of testing. Would the new constitution be observed? The agencies in opposition to the projected revolution in government and conduct had increased in number and strength. Could all the hostile forces be combined? Hildebrand faced a struggle whose issue must either crown or crush his future.

CHAPTER VI.

THE POWER BEHIND THE PAPAL SEE.

THE shadow of Germany yet fell athwart Rome. The proximity of Tuscan and of Norman counted for naught, as the memory arose of the sturdy soldiers who time and again came from over the Alps to alter the fortunes of the Church. Some, however, had grown bold enough after the death of Nicholas II to advise to proceed to an election in defiance of the wishes of the representatives of the emperor. But the attitude of the Imperial Court to those who belonged to the Hildebrandine party decided a course of action for the reformers. The legate of the cardinals was refused an audience, and after five successive days of rejection he returned to Rome, where an election was held on October 1, 1061. The prescribed method was followed, the seven Cardinals making the nomination of Anselm, Bishop of Lucca, who took the name of Alexander II. There was a great throng of begging monks in the city, and their advocacy was intense for Anselm, who had been their patron through the years, and was himself a foremost champion of all the monastic ideals. This spectacle

of a new Primate attended by the hosts of mendi-
cants in their sleeveless habits, adorned by the
odious gourd and sack, called forth the hostile cries
of the populace and of the imperialists. But the
additional escort of hundreds of Norman soldiers,
under the command of Richard of Capua, gave a
constraining hint of the power that sustained the
ordination at St. John's Lateran. Back of it all
the thorough masterful planning of Hildebrand was
unmistakable, and Alexander II at once made him
chancellor of the Roman Church.

The new Pope was the strongest prelate who
could have been selected, aside from the mighty
monk, his manager. The Pataria of Milan had been
the supporters of his reforms, and now a division
of the Lombard strength became possible. His
relations with Germany had ever been friendly, and
in character he was upright and sincere. The
action of the cardinals was interpreted as a formal
challenge to the Empire. The Roman nobles,
changed to be the anti-national party, invited Henry
to send to Rome and assume the office of Patricius,
which had been given to his father, Henry III. A
portion of the city clergy, led by Hugh the White,
joined, through jealousy of Hildebrand, the hostile
barons. The clergy of Milan under the direction of
Guibert, the chancellor of the Empire in Italy, held
a Synod, and memorialized the empress that a Pope
be chosen from their diocese, and one who would
be mercifully inclined to the married brethren.

Agnes proceeded slowly, and finally called a Diet
at Basle for October 28th, which she and her son
of twelve attended. Henry IV was declared
Patricius of Rome, and the German and Lombard
prelates chose for their Pontiff Cadalus, Bishop of
Parma, known as Honorius II. Cadalus was a
supreme object of aversion to all reformers. Peter
Damiani made a characteristic assault upon him,
which portrays vividly the prejudice and vitupera-
tion of the period. Cadalus was branded a preacher
of the devil, an apostle of Antichrist, a root of sin,
the sink of all vices, and food for hellfire. It is not
probable that he was entirely without character or
learning, for he served as a courtier of high repute.
He was rich, but not aggressive, and certainly no
match in ability for his rival and that keen counselor,
the indomitable power behind the Papal See. Germany was tardy in its support of Cadalus, though
its threats against the so-called usurpers were loud.
It was a time for liveliest energy, but the anti-Pope
was left largely to his own resources. Six months
passed before he advanced through Italy, his support
drawn mainly from the Lombards.

Within this time there had been a certain spurious revival of the civic sense in Rome, and an odd
movement executed by Benzo, a bishop of the
Piedmont, who appeared as the ambassador of the
emperor. He was versed in the Italian nature, and
played the part of an ideal religious buffoon and
demagogue. By a series of harangues and a lavish

scattering of gold he secured a following of the masses. Benzo called next a parliament in the renowned Circus Maximus, even then a place of crumbling arches, prostrate obelisks, confused débris, and weeds. But the multitude gathered in its circle of rising seats was made to fancy itself an ancient assembly of the Roman tribes. Alexander II was called to trial, and Benzo, in his invective, charged him with simony, thus counterfeiting the methods of the reformers, and declared that Hildebrand, as the very son of Simon Magus, had been the chief agent in this detestable merchandise. He further denounced the Pope as a traitor to Germany, and ordered in the king's name that he abdicate his office and seek the forgiveness of his sovereign. Alexander had come to the Circus Maximus with an armed retinue, and thus escaped violence. He answered firmly that his election had been received regularly and without taint, and that he was loyal to Henry IV, with whom he would gladly treat. But the Pope, before a packed, excited populace, could not make a very brave showing; and as he rode away, his portion from the mob was jeers and hostile demonstrations. An invitation was extended in the name of the people to Cadalus to come to Rome, so that Benzo left behind him a powerful faction as he went to greet the nominee of the Council of Basle. Guibert, Chancellor of Italy, and a large body of troops formed the retinue of the contesting Pontiff. Alexander believed himself strong enough

for an encounter, even though the Normans had
delayed reinforcements at the critical moment. The
battle of the two claimants to spiritual suzerainty
was joined, on April 14, 1063, north of the city, at
Monte Mario, and the result was a defeat for the
soldiers of the Hildebrandine party. The vanquished
were able to recross the Tiber and intrench themselves behind the city walls, while the victors briefly
held the Leonine section, then retired to the open
plains.

At this juncture Godfrey of Tuscany appeared
in arms as a compulsory arbiter. He chose to be
very politic, and would favor neither claimant; but
they were summarily turned out of the city, each
sent to his respective, original bishopric, one to
Lucca, the other to Parma, and told to await there
the decision of the emperor as to which should be
Pope. Hildebrand, satirized as the Lord of the
Lord Pope, all the while was intensely active. His
adherents must be held together, and he did not
refrain from the use of money, which was furnished
by a generous convert. He was busy trying to form
alliances, and kept in close touch with the progress
of events in Germany. On the issue of the contro-
versies there hinged the settlement of the tangled
Cisalpine affairs. The powerful feudatories did not
approve of the regency of the empress, and the
Church dignitaries had quarreled over the control
of the prince. Henry, Bishop of Augsburg, held
Henry IV as his ward, and was believed also to

exercise undue influence over the mother Agnes. The boy was alleged to be growing up too much of a woman. Accordingly a conspiracy of Anno, Archbishop of Cologne, Siegfried, Archbishop of Mainz, and certain leading barons, resulted in the abduction of the youth. The nation at large was induced to acquiesce in the change of guardians, however much the empress was distressed at the violence and the character of the administration.

Anno brought a reversal in the position of the Empire to the Papacy, for a Council was called at Augsburg, whose deliberations caused a practical abandonment of the cause of Cadalus. The chancellorship of Italy was taken from Guibert, his chief abbot, and given to a reform bishop, Gregory of Vercelli. Alexander was then escorted with a show of authority back to Rome by Godfrey. There was, however, this formidable limitation: the Leonine section was held by the friends of the deposed rival. The barons were his partisans, for they hated the Norman troops who guarded the Pontiff at the Lateran Palace. Cencius, a son of the Prefect of the city, was a constant disturber of the peace. The Lombard clergy continued firm in its allegiance to Cadalus. But at this time an eminent recruit joined the Hildebrandine party. The empress, out of power in Germany and separated from her son, assumed the vows of the religious order. She came to Rome to the Convent of St. Petronilla in great humility, with veil and sackcloth and psalter, and meanly attended. Twelve years earlier, escorted by a brilliant retinue, with her valiant husband, Henry III, Agnes had been crowned at St. Peter's. Her wealth, along with her influence, was now given to Alexander, and she became thenceforth the associate of the Church in its contest with imperialism.

The mastery in Germany next underwent another shift, and the fortunes of Rome were at once affected, just as in the eighteenth century the affairs of the American Colonies reflected promptly all the shades of differences arising between England and France. Anno of Cologne was unable to retain his control over Henry IV, who, with the assistance of the ever-jealous prelates, called Adelbert, Archbishop of Bremen, to be his counselor. He was a man of splendid talents, but fond of display and ambitious of power and wealth. Under his guardianship the prince was left largely to his own devices, and was denied the discipline and preparation that would have equipped him for his future duties. The hostile biographers of Henry IV allege that Adelbert deliberately ruined his ward. The German archbishop encouraged Cadalus to reassert his claim upon the See at Rome. In April, 1063, he again appeared with his troops, and effected a union with Cencius, the castle of St. Angelo becoming the basis of operations. Civil war ensued for more than a year, neither rival gaining a notable advantage over the other. The facilities for intrenchment were abundant; a multitude of massive, fortified palaces became easily available, while every bridge bristled with towers. The money of Cadalus insured a vigorous support. The Norman troops kept Alexander safely in the Lateran. Each hurled at the other all the varieties of Papal anathema; but the schism once more moved to a termination as there came an upheaval again in the ecclesiastical politics of Germany. A widespread, irresistible conspiracy of nobles and Churchmen, a combination so frequently effected in this loosely knit nation, brought the complete downfall of Adelbert, and Anno returned to power. A Council met at Mantua for an investigation of the rights of the claimants. Previous to this Assembly, Anno visited Rome, where he entered into a controversy with Hildebrand. The German chided Alexander for daring to assume the powers of the Papacy without having received the consent of the Northern ruler, saying that this was an absolute condition to the office. Hildebrand replied with firmness, denying this right to have been exercised by the emperors without restrictions or limit of time. He offered proof that once there existed freedom of Papal elections, and asserted, further, that under the circumstances the choice by the College of Cardinals of his master was justified. Yet the Roman chancellor was not strenuous in protesting against the obligation to the emperor, rightly knowing the understanding about to be reached. Two years previous, in the Council at

Augsburg, Peter Damiani had argued for the Papal cause, that during the infancy of Henry IV the right of the emperor to confirm an election was suspended. He said that the Church, occupying the place of a Mother, was the guardian of his spiritual affairs, and thus received the right to choose the Pope. Whatever the merits of the debates, when the session was held at Mantua on May 31, 1064, Alexander was present to defend himself against the formal charge of simony. He was acquitted, and officially acknowledged as the true Pope by the imperial authority. Even this did not put an end to the pretensions of Cadalus. He held out in St. Angelo, on the Tiber, for many months, until, hard pressed, he bought for a large sum of silver the chance to escape to Lombardy, where he died, yet styling himself the Pope Honorius II. The conclusion of the schism was a decided victory for Hildebrand. The fact that his candidate, after six years of struggle, was accepted as the head of the Church gave him an enlarged prestige. He was praised by the writers of the day, and compared in his services to Rome with Marius and Cæsar. The Archbishop of Salerno asked, in an ode, what more Rome owed to the Scipios and other statesmen than it did to Hildebrand. He was intrepid and imperious. Nothing in his remarkable career was more characteristic than his relations with Peter Damiani. This impetuous hermit, who had been drawn from his retreat to a city bishopric and was foremost in every fray for the Church, finally refused high office, and returned to the life of the monastery. He did not agree with all the plans of Hildebrand, yet he was dominated by the chancellor as though he were a mere child. He spoke of Hildebrand as his flattering tyrant, who had soothed him with the pity of a Nero, and had patted him with eagle's claw. On one occasion, when he had been charged with failure to execute orders, Damiani protested his faithfulness, saying that if he deserved death he would lay down his head. He wrote in conclusion: "Strike; but, at the same time, I entreat the holy demon who torments me not to be quite so cruel towards me. Let his venerable arrogance chasten me, not from a distance, but be more gentle towards his slave."

Hildebrand was likewise the director of the enlarged activity that came to the Papacy. Once more Rome figured as the capital of the world, and ambassadors from all parts of Europe, crowded the chambers of the Lateran. Legates went without hindrance to France to decide ecclesiastical disputes. Cardinal Hugh the White, having deserted Cadalus, was the trusted agent of the Church in Spain. The Eastern emperor sent as gifts two brazen gates of rare beauty. These were placed in the Church of St. Paul, and one of them was given the name Hildebrand, the other that of the consul for the year. The chief civil officer in Rome, however, was the Prefect, sometimes named by Germany; at this period, the choice of the people. When the barons were quiescent, a semblance of order prevailed through the city, and the Church for a season escaped the incongruous situation of dominion abroad and pitiful impotence at home. The recognition of Alexander as Primate gave the reformed party a strong impetus. It seemed that the principles for which it had stood were now to be established. The independence of the Church from the State was somewhat nearer an assured fact. A substantial reinforcement had been afforded to the movement for the correction of clerical abuses. The issue was defined with bold clearness. The claims of Cadalus were defended by the lax prelates, so the imperial cause by natural association came to be regarded as that of the anti-reform party. The result was a firmer union of all reformers who were committed to the triumph of principles rather than to the success of an individual.

In 1063, a Synod of Alexander II had enacted the customary decrees against simony and marriage. All of the Papal letters urged rigid adherence to the reformed standards. In Florence the reform spirit took the direction of an attack upon the archbishop as a simoniac. The monks of Vallombrosa were the persistent accusers. The Pope would not allow them to take any definite action, but Hildebrand is believed to have encouraged the remonstrance of the regular clergy. Finally the monks raised an

7

appeal direct to God, as the discerner of all hearts,
and demanded the ordeal by fire to decide whether
their declaration of the guilt of the archbishop was
true.   The populace then joined the cry, and the
authorities had to consent that the test be made.
No device that would awe the witnessing multitude
was neglected.   The very conditions of the trial
emphasized the superstitious belief of the age; for
the provision was that the bishop should not be considered guilty unless the champion of the monks
passed through the mounting flames unharmed.
The outcome of the ordeal can be readily surmised.
The smell of fire was not found upon the garments
of him who henceforth was named Petrus Igneus.
Against such a judgment of heaven the mild and
rather examplary bishop dare not stand, but with-
drew from the city.   A few centuries later, in Florence, a similar clamor of the populace for the ordeal
by fire gave a chance to the enemies of the saintly
Savonarola to turn the occasion into a signal for the
overthrow of the famous reformer.   The wave of
correction spread from Italy even to a few of the
high places in Germany.   The Archbishops Anno
and Siegfried were summoned to Rome to answer
for their irregularities.   Their ready acceptance of
the Papal right to bring them to judgment, along
with the certainty of their guilt of simony, led
Alexander to pronounce forgiveness, and dismiss
them with the adjuration to sin no more.   The complaints which continued to be lodged against

Siegfried indicated that his repentance, at least, was very brief.

The emperor likewise felt the weight of the new authority at Rome, when he ventured to secure a divorce from Bertha of Susa. His marriage with the family of Savoy had been arranged by his father, and only at the urgent solicitation of his advisers did the union take place. Henry formed a violent aversion to his wife, and after two years of wedlock declared his purpose to obtain a separation. His nobles did not dare to speak in opposition, but at the Council called in Mainz to take the necessary steps, the redoubtable Peter Damiani appeared as the apostolic legate. His condemnation of the proposed divorce was unsparing, and the emperor was warned that if he did not abandon his plan the powers of the canon law would be turned against him. Under such leadership the real sentiment of the court risked expression, and Henry had to recognize the dominion of the Church. Later the true womanliness of Bertha, and her fidelity to her liege lord under all conditions of fortune, won a measure of appreciation from her husband. On the other hand, the relations of Henry with his subjects grew more and more strained. Otto of Nordheim, Duke of Bavaria, broke into open revolt, but was vanquished. The emperor distrusted Rudolf, Duke of Suabia, and goaded him to hostility. Territory in Saxony was seized and powerfully garrisoned. The seeds of discontent and resentment were scattered broadcast, and the young ruler found his government growing weak and unstable, while the structure of the Roman hierarchy continued to rise in power and majesty. The rehabilitation of the Papacy and its influence over the affairs of England was equally important.

Another Norman Duke looked to Rome for a sanction of his conquests. This was William, who ruled along the Seine in Northern France. However shadowy were his claims upon the succession across the channel, when once the Pope had confirmed it, his title took a validity that condoned all rapine and bloodshed. Hildebrand, led by his usual Churchly statecraft, was the spokesman for William, and gained by his arguments the support of the cardinals for the invasion. The insular Church under the Saxons had been slow to respond to the directions of the Holy See, while Norman supremacy would bring a close union with the Continent. The consecrated banner sent by Alexander bore speedy fruits in the victory at Hastings, which was followed by a general revival of church-building and a vigorous ecclesiastical reorganization. Lanfranc, as Archbishop of Canterbury, sent to the Pope for the pallium, but was constrained to come to Rome to receive it. Many honors were shown him, for Lanfranc was an influential advocate of the most extensive powers of the Papacy. Opportune adjustments now occurred in the Italian situation. Duke Godfrey had equaled in authority the emperor himself. Though the agent of Germany, through the influence of his wife Beatrice, he was not unfriendly to the Church. But his policy had been cautious and frequently neutral. At Christmas, 1069, he died, and his widow survived him six years.

The foremost figure of the day and the mightiest woman of many centuries, Matilda, the great countess, the daughter of Beatrice, became henceforth the invaluable ally of the Hildebrandine cause. She had married a son of her stepfather Godfrey, known as Godfrey the Hunchback. It was a political match, and proved uncongenial. Godfrey the younger was a devoted supporter of Henry IV, and in a few years turned his back upon his wife and Italy for Germany. She had received the most liberal culture, and possessed a rich diversity of talents. She was as capable in administration as she was profound in learning, and devoted to the Church. Her personality expresses itself in the way she was wont to inscribe her name, "Matilda, by the Grace of God what I am." Her spirit was ardent, and her sympathies intense, so that the incomparable genius of Hildebrand might well throw its most potent spell over such a nature and intelligence as Matilda's. The character and purpose of the monk of Cluny commanded such an allegiance as only a similar lofty and imperious spirit could recognize and render. A personal friendship, pure and complete, entirely without parallel, existed between the champion of the Church and its consistent communicant. However large was the measure of individual and moral support which the great countess gave the reform party, the material resources which she had placed at the control of the Pontiff were the absolute essentials for winning the spiritual supremacy.

The counsels of Peter Damiani ceased in 1072, after he had made his last public appearance with the Pope and Hildebrand at the dedication of the splendid basilica at Monte Cassino. To this gathering came the Norman counts of the South and many prelates of Italy. It was a significant demonstration of the strength which Rome had attained, and a pledge of the independence with which its new career would be pursued. For the intervention of Germany had taught the Papacy to stand alone.

After a Pontificate of twelve years, on April 31, 1073, Alexander passed away. A survey of his career gives the impression that he had been better served than serving. He was so largely overshadowed by the powerful Hildebrand that he seems to lack personality and force. His disposition was mild, but his courage was steady, for he had ever been a consistent advocate of the reform ideas of his age. Twenty-five years of waiting and training had fallen to the lot of the mightiest man of the Church. Was the monk now ready and equipped to surrender the place of counselor and assume the momentous responsibilities of the Apostolic See?

CHAPTER VII.

THE PLAN OF THE MASTER-BUILDER.

UPON the occasion of the death of a Pope, the populace of Rome had a practice of sacking the Papal palace and of rioting about the city. Hildebrand now saw in grateful surprise, as a token of the new authority won by the Church, that the citizens were peaceful and orderly. As chancellor and archdeacon, it was his duty to appoint three days of fasting and prayer, after which the College of Cardinals would conduct its election. What Churchman must receive the lofty honor needed scarcely to be asked, yet it came as an astounding climax that the narrowly prescribed method of choice was to be violated in behalf of the very reformer who had created it.

The funeral services of Alexander II were being conducted on the day after his death with stately pomp in the Church of St. John Lateran, by Hildebrand, when suddenly the ceremonies were interrupted by a multitude of the lesser clergy and the people, who came thronging into the sanctuary, and began to shout the name of Hildebrand. The cries increased, "Let Hildebrand be bishop." "The

Blessed Peter wills the Archdeacon Hildebrand to be Pope." In vain did the one so tumultuously proclaimed endeavor to quell the clamor of his admirers. It appeared that the voice of the people was truly to be the voice of God. When Hildebrand tried to mount one of the pulpits to enforce his exhortation, he was put aside by the cardinal presbyter, Hugh the White, who became, in the mind of of the Assembly, the interpreter of the will of the cardinals. "Brethren," he said, "ye know, and as it appears, acknowledge, how, since the days of Leo IX, Hildebrand hath proven himself a man of discretion and probity; how he hath exalted the dignity of our Roman Church, and rescued our city from most imminent dangers. As it is impossible to find a better man, or, indeed, his equal, to intrust with the future defense of our Church and State, we therefore, the cardinal bishops, do, with one voice, elect Hildebrand to be your spiritual pastor and our own." Then, according to the personal record left by the Pope-elect, the mob rushed upon him in a kind of frenzy, and bore him to the Church of S. Pietro in Vinculo. Here they placed upon him the Papal robe of scarlet, and put upon his head the miter of two golden circlets, the crown royal bestowed by God, and the crown imperial, given by the hand of Peter. Lastly they led him to the apostolic throne, "unwilling and sad," as one narrative reads. The decree of election from the cardinals was in readiness, and was pronounced before the enthusiastic and applauding public. Its eulogy bore handsome tribute to the career then being crowned. The document declared that "We choose for our pastor and Pontiff a devout man; one mighty in human and divine knowledge; a distinguished lover of equity and justice; a man firm in adversity and temperate in prosperity; a man, according to the saying of the apostle, of good behavior, blameless, modest, sober, chaste, given to hospitality, and one that ruleth well his own house; a man from his childhood brought up in the bosom of this Mother Church, and for the merit of his life already raised to the archidiaconal dignity. We choose, namely, our Archdeacon Hildebrand to be Pope and successor to the Apostle, and to bear henceforth and forever the name of Gregory." Then the shout of the multitude echoed as a benediction, "St. Peter has chosen our Lord Gregory Pope."

In such fashion again the ancient custom of popular election asserted itself, with a conventional sanction to be given by the higher authorities. It is fruitless to inquire whether the whole affair was not a deliberate plan to which Hildebrand was a party, or rather a spontaneous outburst of all interests which turned irresistibly to him for guidance. He was the logical man of the hour. His title to genuine greatness rests on the fact that he had been the most potent agent in bringing to pass the situation then prevailing in Church affairs. He alone could prosecute the issue and be the master of the future. His temper of mind at this time is most interesting to study. There was a real shrinking from the duties he must discharge. "Sad and unwilling" was possibly the condition of the flesh, but certainly not of the spirit of this dauntless leader. He passed some days in retirement, from which he told his intimate friends the feelings of his inmost soul. To Desiderius, the Abbot of Monte Cassino, he wrote in the phrase of the psalmist: "I am come into deep waters, where the floods overflow me. I am weary of my crying; my throat is dried. Fearfulness and trembling are come upon me, and horror hath overwhelmed me." Guibert of Ravenna, who was unfriendly, was implored, "Let your affection be shown forth, if not for my merits, at least for the love of the Apostles Peter and Paul. Call on the sons of Jesus Christ to entreat God for me that He may give me strength to sustain the burden He has laid upon me in spite of my refusal." He announced his election to the Countesses Beatrice and Matilda, to the King of Denmark, the Archbishop of Rheims, and Hugh, Abbot of Cluny, and besought their support of him in prayers and sympathy.

The chief perils of his day mentioned were the sins and injustice of rulers and the selfishness and apostasy of the clergy. He called to the Archbishop of Canterbury to see how fearful it would be for him to abstain from opposing such persons, and again how difficult to oppose them. In another epistle he stated his rule of action: "We may not set aside the law of God through respect of persons, nor swerve from the path of right for the sake of human favor. As the Apostle says: 'If I should wish to please men, I should not be the servant of God.'" Notwithstanding, then, the appearance of inability to enter into his high office, no Pontiff ever had at his installation such a clean-cut program and well-defined aims.

The quarter of a century of diplomacy and administration for his superiors had brought Hildebrand a profound knowledge of the temporal affairs of Europe, of the centers of influence at work and the resources available. Gregory VII began his rule as the heir of all the claims of Papal dominion advanced in the centuries past, as the defender of all that was ascetic and uncompromising in the religious practice of his day, and as the champion of a sovereignty that allowed no element of control save the sacerdotal. But first a reckoning must be made with the emperor. A notification of the election was sent him, and the ceremony of consecration deferred until some evidence of the attitude of Henry was secured. The German and Lombard bishops urged him to interpose his objection, for they fearfully and properly anticipated that the severity of the archdeacon against delinquents would be continued in the greater rigor of the Primate. But imperial affairs were not in a position to enter a contest with the Roman Church, and an ambassador was sent to learn the circumstances of the succession. The inquiry was a mere matter of form, and the chancellor of the Empire for Italy was present officially when Hildebrand was consecrated Pope on June 29, 1073, more than two months after his election.

The relations of Henry and Hildebrand supply the motive to all the triumphs and defeats of this Pontificate. The king had been condemned by Alexander for certain practices, but Gregory VII was not disposed to judge harshly in advance, though his attitude would be uncompromising. To Duke Godfrey he declared that no one was more solicitous than he for the king's temporal and eternal welfare. He intended to counsel with Henry, and would rejoice if he acquiesced in the things touching the Church and himself. But if hatred were returned for love, the Pope said, he would not incur the curse pronounced on him "who keepeth back his sword from blood." To the Countess Beatrice, Hildebrand wrote: "It is our wish to send religious men to the king to recall him to the love of his mother, the Holy Roman Church, and to a becoming mode of governing his Empire. If he refuse to listen to us, it were more safe for us to resist him, if necessary, even to the pouring forth of our blood, for the sake of his salvation, than yielding to his will, to rush to destruction with him." The response of Henry to Rome was amazing in its humility. Hildebrand spoke of it as a letter full of sweetness and obedience, and such as never had been sent by any emperor to the Church authorities. He confessed his past transgressions and threw himself upon the Papal indulgence. He said the Church of Milan was in error through his fault, and prayed that it be reformed with other Churches. Henry promised that, "by God's grace, we will be wanting to you in nothing, and we solicit in return the exercise of a parental care over us in all things." Again, at Canossa, he will make a similar and even more complete surrender.

At this time, September, 1073, the troubled circumstances of Germany throw some light on the emperor's desire for peace in Italy. Too frequently the deeds of these two pitted champions of the State and the Church were not in harmony with their professions. Each exercised his skill in using words to darken counsel and avoid the real issue of controversy. For the future the alternatives to them were a truce or a conflict. The official duties of Hildebrand had been assumed before the recognition of Henry was tendered. They consisted notably of a series of embassies and communications to the various nations. The keynote of his administration was at once sounded in a radical and bold departure. Leo IX and other Pontiffs had been concerned to recover and hold the lands gained in the alleged donations of Charlemagne and Pepin; but the vision of this imperious successor of St. Peter did not confine itself to Italian territory, but expanded to the sovereignty of the world. Hildebrand had kept his ambitious desires in restraint and bided his time. Such was the power of the Church over the mediæval mind that the assertion of secular dominion was not received as something untenable. The view of the nature of Christ's kingdom on earth had come to be materialized, just as the Jews in the days of Jesus of Nazareth expected a political incarnation of their religion by a Messiah. Under this confusion, demands could not be made which were spiritually the due of the Church and its precepts without also claiming for it a civil preeminence. Specifically, the supreme authority was based on the doctrine that Christ was the Lord of the earth, and the Pope, as His sole vicar, shared His prerogatives. There was much of unrest and change in political affiliations, which contributed to further the aggressive claims of the Papacy.

The first embassy of Hildebrand went to Spain under Hugh the White, who worked to promote the unity of the Church through the adoption of the Roman ritual. But, further, the princes of Spain were told that their land of old belonged to St. Peter, and yet remained the property of the Apostolic See. If they wished to wrest any possessions from the Moors, they must hold them as fiefs of Rome. The payment was a small annual tribute, and some of the lesser rulers found such acknowledgment helpful to the consolidation of their power. Later, similar claims were advanced over Sardinia,

Corsica, Dalmatia, Poland, Scandinavia, and England. In not a few instances, princes sought such a protectorate from motives of self-interest rather than of pious obedience. Pretenders have been described in these pages, and others imitated them, who, in order to make sure their rule, gladly offered their lands in fealty to the Pope. But the demands of Hildebrand were sometimes resisted.

Particularly was the Pope anxious to have the political support of the Normans. Robert Guiscard had largely grown in power, and was loath to renew his allegiance to Rome. Hildebrand visited Southern Italy to meet him, but all appointments were evaded, and the crafty warrior failed to come to terms. The Prince of Capua and the Duke of Benevento, who made the feudal acknowledgment, were accordingly favored and intrigued for to the detriment of the Prince of Apulia. The disaffection of Robert Guiscard led the Pope in his restless energy to originate the plan of the heroic enterprise which engaged all Europe for several succeeding generations. He received in his first year from the Emperor Michael of Constantinople, an appeal to enlist Western Christendom against the advancing Seljuk Turks, with a hint that the Greek and Roman Churches might be eventually united. This call seemed to give an opportunity to rally the enthusiasm of believers for a grand assault upon the East under the command of Rome. The success of military adventure would be made to contribute to the political absolutism of the hierarchy. Hildebrand accordingly dispatched a favorable envoy to the Eastern Empire, and summoned several of the faithful feudal barons to collect troops for a movement against the infidels. In March, 1074, the news came that the Saracens had appeared before the walls of Constantinople. Promptly the Pope issued a formal appeal to all Christians to rise to deliver their brethren in the East from the power of the infidels. He admonished all believers that as the Redeemer of the world had given His life for His servants, each of them should be willing to offer up his own for those of the faith. The crowning significance of such a crusade was the ultimate design of not only rescuing the Greeks, who were under the ban of insubordination to Rome, but also of replacing them under the Papal authority. The response of the rulers came tardily and feebly. Some were reprimanded for entire neglect to obey; others refused to serve in company with their hereditary enemies. The Countess of Tuscany was prevented from furnishing the promised quota of thirty thousand men by an insurrection. The immediate subtle object of this military mustering, which was ordered for South Italy, was to intimidate the threatening Robert Guiscard, who had been excommunicated on account of his invasions. The miscarriage of these plans filled the Pope with humiliation, and threw him into a severe illness. This was accompanied by an intense despondency

of spirit, an experience common to him after periods
of exaltation and enthusiasm. He felt that good-
ness had all but fled from the earth and few were
true to their religious responsibilities. He wrote
that he "had hoped to escape to that country where
repose is prepared for the weary."

But buoyancy and jubilant recovery followed
speedily, and in December, 1074, he was more hope-
ful than before of a mighty crusade. He informed
Henry IV that more than fifty thousand men were
ready to rise against the enemies of God and march
by the guidance of the Lord to His holy sepulcher,
if he as Pontiff would put himself at their head.
He asked the emperor to give him aid, and com-
mended the chief care of the Church to Germany
in his absence. Such was the daring genius of this
vicar of the Prince of Peace who would have taken
carnal arms for the conquest of men's souls. Yet all
of this stir was chimerical. The levies faded away,
while only Tuscany was loyal. Europe, as a whole,
was indifferent to the project, and the Emperor
Michael was deposed at Constantinople. A religious
war in the East was impossible, while the independence of the Church in the West was still uncertain.
But who shall say how largely the faith and interest
of Gregory VII in the Holy Land contributed to
the enlisting of the myriad hosts at the close of
the century? His spirit-stirring exhortations lived
again in the eloquence of Urban II and the zeal of
Peter the Hermit. Hildebrand and the Crusader

8

possessed a common bond in their lofty vision and
ascetic temper.

The new administration, chosen solely with
reference to reform, did not begin its expected
measures until the eleventh month of its first year,
in Lent. Three guiding ideas mark the career of
Hildebrand: that the Church should be one and
Rome its head; that the Church should be free; and
that the Church should be pure. Before his Pontificate none of these had been realized, though ecclesiastical freedom was vastly promoted by the
method of election adopted in 1059. The means
for the purification of the Church and the renewal
of the hierarchy were very clear and simple to his
mind, but many powerful ones would offer a thousand obstacles to his policy. The worst foes were of
his own household. The clergy did not want to
be reformed. But Hildebrand had no fear of the
outcome. He did not shrink from the contest when
once it was begun. His cause, in his belief, was
ever that of righteousness. All the efforts of mortals
must be futile against the decrees of St. Peter and
the power of the Lord God. The summons for the
Council at Rome was issued in January, 1074, and
the Papal opinion of the critical nature of affairs was
indicated in a letter to the Archbishop of Aquileia.
It reads: "The princes of this world, seeking only
their own interest and not that of Jesus Christ, treat
the Church like a vile slave. The priests and visible
rulers of the Church evade the law of God and

their obligation to Him and to their flocks. They seek the dignities of the Church solely for the sake of the worldly glory, and they consume in useless expense that which should be devoted to the salvation of the many. The people, whom the teaching of the prelates does not lead into the way of justice, but who are rather taught evil by the example of their leaders, fall into all sorts of crimes. They have the name of Christians, not only without fulfilling a Christian duty, but also without even keeping the faith. Wherefore, trusting in the mercy of God, we have resolved to assemble a Synod to find a remedy for so many evils, so that we may not witness in our day the irreparable ruin and destruction of the Church." The German and Lombard bishops did not attend the Synod, but the Countess Matilda was present and participated. Four decrees were adopted. No one who had been admitted to any rank in the ministry by a payment should be allowed to officiate. No one who had purchased any Church should retain it, and no one in the future should buy or sell ecclesiastical rights. All who lived in the married state should cease to exercise the clerical function. That none of the laity should receive the ministrations of those who destroyed these ordinances. Thus the reformation was inaugurated with a rigor and a thoroughness befitting the spirit of an Elijah. Endless declarations had been made by Councils against simony. The celibacy of all priests was an ideal condition to

be preached about and favored in ecclesiastical
resolutions; but the marriage of the secular clergy
had grown to be the rule rather than the exception.
If Hildebrand now were merely a politician, he
would not have incited the furious enmity of thou-
sands by an attack upon their marital relations.
Instead, he was set on effecting that in which the
Council of Nicæa itself had failed. A separation
was to ensue such as the world had not seen since
the command of Ezra went forth in Judea.

A new method was called into play by the Synod
of 1074 in the place assigned to the laity, for they
became the executors of its statutes. The sacraments performed by simoniacal or married priests
were henceforth to be refused. The mighty weapon
of public opinion, very sparingly employed under
mediævalism, was invoked to supplement the thun-
der of the anathemas of the Church against the
guilty. The religious standards of the people
naturally made stern exactions of the priests, and
the monks everywhere were ready for a relentless
propaganda of reform. But the opposition was immediate and violent, especially in respect to the
obligation of celibacy. Otho of Constance and other
bishops of Germany combined to resist it. The
Archbishop of Mainz feared to promulgate the laws
until after six months, and then his suffragans refused to listen to him, and left the assembly. In
France there was equally vehement antagonism; for
the Archbishop of Rouen, when he attempted to

enforce the act against marriage, was pelted with stones and fled in despair. A Synod at Paris renounced obedience to the decrees, and the one advocate of the reforms was beaten and thrown into prison. In Spain, the Papal legate, the Abbot of Marseilles, was met with violence when he tried to secure their adoption at the Council of Burgos. Guibert of Ravenna rallied the hosts of the malcontents in Lombardy. Lanfranc in England did not even consider these radical principles for a period of time; but the Council of Winchester, in 1076, decided that thereafter no married person should be admitted to orders. But Hildebrand was not stopped by any of these failures. His exhortation was, "Fear not; despair not; extinguish simony and enforce celibacy, and God will uphold you." To the people of Franconia he sent warning that, by the apostolic authority, they should refuse the ministrations of all condemned priests, whatever their bishops may say to the contrary.

In France the practice of simony was flagrantly prevalent. The Pope addressed the chief prelate of the land, Manasses of Rheims, in an unusual accusation. He charged that the king was the instigator of a series of heinous crimes against man and Church, and the ministry of France was responsible for it, since his actions had not been resisted and preached against. The archbishop was directed to warn King Philip of his own and the kingdom's danger, and tell him that if he refused to heed, the

anathema of the Church would be visited upon him.
If that failed to move him, Hildebrand pledged
himself to tear the kingdom from his possession.
But Manasses was a relative of the royal family,
and not likely to proceed against its head; while
Philip was not affected by the fulminations from
Rome. The Pope, after two years' zealous effort,
concluded in an epistle to his friend Hugh, Abbot
of Cluny, that the religious situation had not been
improved. He wrote: "In the regions of the East,
the South, and the North, scarcely any bishops are
lawfully admitted to their office, nor do they lead
lives conformable to their sacred character. Among
the secular princes there are none who prefer God's
honor to their own, or righteousness to gain. Those
nations among whom I dwell are in some sense
worse than Jews or pagans." By reason of such
a grievous indictment of society, Hildebrand decided to assemble another Synod. In the call to
the convocation, the unfortunate troubles in the
Church and the unbridled audacity of its enemies
were named as its causes. The Pontiff hoped to
force the emperor to renounce his undertaking
against the Saxons, and to settle the Christian religion in its original liberty and peace. German
affairs had grown critically complicated since the
day Henry sent his contrite letter to Rome. The
suspicions against Saxony, encouraged by Adelbert
of Bremen, developed into open hostility. The
aggressions, begun under the pretext of the dis-

loyalty of its duke, aroused the readily turbulent
inhabitants. The Saxons made formal charges
against the personal character of the king and the
evil influence of his counselors. They even endeavored to have a National Assembly meet to
depose Henry. The bishops friendly to him were
driven from the duchy, and the conflict partook of
the nature of a religious war. The uncertain ties
of feudalism prevented the king from relying upon
his imperial vassals to help crush the disaffection.
Instead, the opposition spread more widely, and for
a season Henry appeared to be without power or
resources. The Pope was eager to intervene, and
thus sit in judgment.

At last Henry levied sufficient troops to enable
him to treat with the Saxons, and he agreed to
surrender the castles which he held. When this
condition was slowly executed, a great uprising
of the people, in February, 1074, gained the strong-
holds with violence and plunder. Then the king
demanded the condemnation of the rebels by the
Pope; but Hildebrand was intent only upon the
campaign for clerical purity. It has been hostilely
charged that Rome had incited the Saxons. A re-
vulsion of feeling now followed in Germany. Henry
won many of the princes to his support. Those
Churchmen who fell under the condemnation of
Rome became the advocates henceforth of the imperial cause. Hildebrand urged the Dukes of
Suabia and Carinthia not to obey their priests, and

this led to a remonstrance from the leading prelates. Two Papal legates endeavored to have a Synod called in Germany to enforce the decrees against simony and marriage; but this aroused the latent sentiment of the National Church, and it was declared no Synod should meet in the presence of Roman legates. Henry personally seemed favorable to such a meeting, though at the same time, with his increasing strength, he pushed his preparations for regaining his authority in Saxony.

At this juncture the second Synod met in Rome, the first week in Lent, February 23-25, 1075. Over fifty bishops were present, with a large company of abbots and priests. All were fervently committed to reform, and no unfriendly prelates were in attendance as in the previous year. Certain bishops of Lombardy and Germany were suspended from their offices. Five counselors of Henry were voted to be excommunicated unless they came to Rome for absolution before June. A similar sentence was threatened against the King of France. The former decrees of the Church against simony and marriage were renewed. A never-relaxing hand had taken the weapons of extermination, and the active alliance of the laity was to win the day. A priest of Treves has given a dark picture of the results of the zeal of the people. The secular priests were frequently brought to extreme poverty, and wandered about without parishes. Many of them were assaulted and foully wounded. The fate of the unfortunate wives was often most direful, and not a few of them took their own lives. The unusual liberty accorded to the communicants led them to despise the sacraments, and the offices of religion were neglected in many places, so that even the dying were denied the last consolations of their faith. Movements for reform of whatever nature, whether wise or unwise, have ever been marked by the excesses of the multitude, who, vaguely conscious of the real issue, conduct themselves with passion and violence. The non-marriage of all clergy, however, after many desperate struggles, came to be the imperative law, and has prevailed through the centuries, a monument to the inflexible purpose of Hildebrand. Its influence upon the Papal system is inestimable; for celibacy has contributed largely that which is essential and distinctive in the Roman Church. Against the law forbidding simony, the princes and bishops did not dare protest. The guilt of such a charge was always denied, however suspicious the circumstances, and the public expression was uniformly abhorrent of all who benefited by the practice. But the sale of offices for a consideration could not be eradicated for all time. The consistency and right living of all Christians, official and laical, made the conditions of the holding of benefices the problem of each succeeding age. Yet the ambitious genius of Hildebrand believed it had now conceived a sovereign remedy against simony and all clerical abuses.

The startling and revolutionary work of the
Synod of 1075 is found in another decree in addition to the customary reform legislation. It was
enacted that: "If any one shall from henceforth
receive a bishopric or abbey from the hand of any
lay person, let him not be reckoned among bishops
or abbots, nor let the privilege of audience be
granted to him as to a bishop or abbot. We more-
over deny to such one the favor of St. Peter and
an entrance into the Church until he shall have
resigned the dignity which he has obtained, both
by the crime of ambition and of disobedience, which
is idolatry. And in like manner do we decree con-
cerning the lesser dignitaries of the Church. Also,
if any emperor, duke, marquis, count, or any secular
person or house whatsoever, shall presume to give
investiture, let him know himself to be bound by the
force of the same sentence." Thus by one stroke
the Church was to cut free from the State, and
any official conferring of clerical dignities by the
laymen was to be punished with excommunication.
It was a decree destined to furnish the two dominant forces of the eleventh century with a battlefield
upon which was waged a contest to rival, if not
surpass, the Thirty Years' War.

A final conclusion of the issue may be considered
not to have been reached until the utterance of the
Golden Bull in 1356, with Germany divorced from
the Papacy. Europe had been long cast in the
mold of feudalism, and the first deadly blow struck